JAMES EARL
JONES

OVERCOMING ADVERSITY

JAMES EARL JONES

Judy L. Hasday, Ed.M.

Introduction by James Scott Brady,
Trustee, the Center to Prevent Handgun Violence
Vice Chairman, the Brain Injury Foundation

Chelsea House Publishers
Philadelphia

*For those who came before and for those who will follow...
dedicated to my family.*
— In loving memory of Ervin Fairbanks

Frontis: James Earl Jones as author Terence Mann in the 1989 film
Field of Dreams.

CHELSEA HOUSE PUBLISHERS

EDITORIAL DIRECTOR Stephen Reginald
PRODUCTION MANAGER Pamela Loos
MANAGING EDITOR Jim Gallagher
PICTURE EDITOR Judy Hasday
ART DIRECTOR Sara Davis
SENIOR PRODUCTION EDITOR Lisa Chippendale

Staff for **James Earl Jones**
SENIOR EDITOR Therese De Angelis
ASSOCIATE ART DIRECTOR Takeshi Takahashi
DESIGNER Keith Trego
PICTURE RESEARCHER Patricia Burns
COVER ILLUSTRATION Earl Parker

3 5 7 9 8 6 4 2

Library of Congress Cataloging-in-Publication Data

Hasday, Judy L., 1957–
James Earl Jones / Judy L. Hasday.
128 pp.   cm. — (Overcoming adversity)
Includes bibliographical references and index.
Summary: Examines the life and career of the successful actor, James Earl
Jones, who overcame a severe problem as a stutterer to become one of the most
recognizable voices in entertainment.
ISBN 0-7910-4702-4. — ISBN 0-7910-4703-2 (pbk.)
1. Jones, James Earl—Juvenile literature. 2. Actors—United States—Biogra-
phy—Juvenile literature. [1. Jones, James Earl. 2. Actors and actresses.
3. Afro-Americans—Biography.] I. Title. II. Series.
PN2287.J589H37 1998
792'.028'092—dc21
[B]   97-31919
                                                                CIP
                                                                 AC

CONTENTS

OVERCOMING ADVERSITY

TIM ALLEN
comedian/performer

MAYA ANGELOU
author

APOLLO 13 MISSION

DREW BARRYMORE
actress

DREW CAREY
comedian/performer

JIM CARREY
comedian/performer

BILL CLINTON
U.S. President

TOM CRUISE
actor

MICHAEL J. FOX
actor

WHOOPI GOLDBERG
comedian/performer

EKATERINA GORDEEVA
figure skater

SCOTT HAMILTON
figure skater

JAMES EARL JONES
actor

QUINCY JONES
composer

ABRAHAM LINCOLN
U.S. President

WILLIAM PENN
Pennsylvania's founder

ROSEANNE
entertainer

SAMMY SOSA
baseball player

DAVE THOMAS
entrepreneur

ROBIN WILLIAMS
comedian/performer

ON FACING ADVERSITY

James Scott Brady

I guess it's a long way from a Centralia, Illinois, train yard to the George Washington University Hospital Trauma Unit. My dad was a yardmaster for the old Chicago, Burlington & Quincy Railroad. As a child, I used to get to sit in the engineer's lap and imagine what it was like to drive that train. I guess I always have liked being in the "driver's seat."

Years later, however, my interest turned from driving trains to driving campaigns. In 1979, former Texas governor John Connally hired me as a press secretary in his campaign for the American presidency. We lost the Republican primary to a former Hollywood star named Ronald Reagan. But I managed to jump over to the Reagan campaign. When Reagan was elected in 1980, I was "sitting in the catbird seat," as humorist James Thurber would say—poised to be named presidential press secretary. I held that title throughout the eight years of the Reagan administration. But not without one terrible, extended interruption.

It happened barely two months after the Reagan administration took office. I never even heard the shots. On March 30, 1981, my life went blank in an instant. In an attempt to assassinate President Reagan, John Hinckley Jr. armed himself with a "Saturday night special"—a low-quality, $29 pistol—and shot wildly as our presidential entourage exited a Washington hotel. One of the exploding bullets struck me just above the left eye. It shattered into a couple dozen fragments, some of which penetrated my skull and entered my brain.

The next few months of my life were a nightmare of repeated surgery, broken contact with the outside world, and a variety of medical complications. More than once, I was very close to death.

The next few years were filled with frustrating struggles to function with a paralyzed right side, struggles to speak and communicate.

To people who face and defeat daunting obstacles, "ambition" is not becoming wealthy or famous or winning elections or awards. Words like "ambition" and "achievement" and "success" take on very different meanings. The objective is just to live, to wake up every morning. The goals are not lofty; they are very ordinary.

My own heroes are ordinary folks—but they accomplish extraordinary things because they try. My greatest hero is my wife, Sarah. She's accomplished a lot of things in life, but two stand out. The first has been the way she has cared for me and our son since I was shot. A tremendous tragedy and burden was dropped unexpectedly into her life, totally beyond her control and without justification. She could have given up; instead, she focused her energies on preserving our family and returning our lives to normal as much as possible. Week by week, month by month, year by year, she has not reached for the miraculous, just for the normal. Yet in focusing on the normal, she has helped accomplish the miraculous.

Her other most remarkable accomplishment, to me, has been spearheading the effort to keep guns out of the hands of criminals and children in America. Opponents call her a "gun grabber"; I call her a national hero. And I am not alone.

After a seven-year battle, during which Sarah and I worked tirelessly to educate the public about the need for stronger gun laws, the Brady Bill became law in 1993. It was a victory, achieved in the face of tremendous opposition, that now benefits all Americans. From the time the law took effect through fall 1997, background checks had stopped 173,000 criminals and other high-risk purchasers from buying handguns, and the law has helped to reduce illegal gun trafficking.

Sarah was not pursuing fame, or even recognition. She simply started at one point—when our son, Scott, found a loaded handgun on the seat of a pickup truck and, thinking it was a toy, pointed it at Sarah.

Fortunately, no one was hurt. But seeing a gun nearly bring a second tragedy upon our family, Sarah became determined to do whatever she could to prevent senseless death and injury from guns.

Some people think of Sarah as a powerful political force. To me, she's the person who so many times fed me and helped me dress during my long years of recovery.

Overcoming obstacles is part of life, not just for people who are challenged by disabilities, illnesses, or tragedies, but for all people. No matter what the obstacle—fear, disability, prejudice, grief, or a difficulty that isn't likely to "just go away"—we can all work to make this world a better place.

1

THE VOICE OF COMMUNICATION

"The speaker's last concern should be how he sounds. The listener, not the speaker, should be aware of how the voice sounds. The speaker should be concerned with what he seeks to communicate by the sound of his voice."

—James Earl Jones, *Voices and Silences*

	VIDEO	AUDIO
Fade in:	Long shot (LS) of man standing on planks leading out to a lake. He has his back to the camera as he tosses a stone into the lake. He turns to face the camera holding a book.	Fade up banjo music sound effect of water plop
Dissolve to:	Medium close-up (MCU) of him tapping on book—holds out in front of him and says	*"This is the book that got Bubba cooked."*
Cut to:	LS of man walking down the street; he waves to truck driving by.	*"This is the man who read an ad . . .*

11

Cut to:	Close-up (CU) of Yellow Pages cover	*that ran in the book that got Bubba cooked."*
Cut to:	LS of fishing supply interior; man from street walks in.	*"This is the store that sold to the man*
Cut to:	CU of man and store clerk talking	*. . . who read an ad that ran*
Cut to:	CU of Yellow Pages book being flipped through	*. . . in the book that got Bubba cooked."*
Cut to:	Medium shot (MS) of man in power boat going across screen on lake	*"This is the lake next to the store . . .*
Cut to:	CU of Yellow Pages book being flipped back to front cover	*with an ad in the book . . .*
Cut to:	MS of man in power boat throwing fishing line into lake	*that got Bubba cooked."*
Rack focus to:	CU of fishing lure and very large fish swimming by	*"And this . . . is Bubba."*
Cut to:	CU of Bell Logo on book	*"The genuine Bell of Pennsylvania . . .*
Cut to:	CU of Bell of Pennsylvania spine	
Cut to:	MS of title on front cover	*"No other book can match it."*
Cut to:	MS of additional type on cover	
Cut to:	CU of Bell Atlantic logo	*"A Bell Atlantic Company."*
Fade to Black		Fade out music

—from the Bell Atlantic commercial spot "Bubba"

A man is sitting on the bleachers along the first baseline of a baseball diamond in a farmer's cornfield. A number of ball players are warming up, catching, hitting balls to one another. The man is Terence Mann, a novelist, and the fate of the ball field is in question. He turns to speak to Ray, the owner of the property:

> People will come, Ray. They'll come to Iowa for reasons they can't even fathom. They'll turn up your driveway not knowing for sure why they're doing it. They'll arrive at your door, as innocent as children, longing for the past. "Of course we won't mind if you look around," you'll say. "It's only $20 per person." They'll pass over the money without even thinking about it, for it is money they have and peace they like. And they'll walk out to the bleachers and sit in shirtsleeves on a perfect afternoon. They'll find they have reserved seats somewhere along one of the base-lines, where they sat when they were children and cheered their heroes. And they'll watch the game, and it'll be as if they dipped themselves in magic waters. The memories will be so thick they'll have to brush them away from their faces. People will come, Ray. The one constant through all the years, Ray, has been baseball. America has rolled by like an army of steamrollers. It's been erased like a black-board, rebuilt, and erased again. But baseball has marked the time. This field, this game, is a part of our past, Ray. It reminds us of all that once was good, and that could be again. Oh, people will come, Ray. People will most defi-nitely come.

—from the motion picture *Field of Dreams*

DARTH VADER: There is no escape [young Skywalker]. Don't make me destroy you. You do not yet realize your importance. You have only begun to discover your power. Join me and I will complete your training. With our com-bined strength, we can end this destructive conflict and bring order to the galaxy.

—from the motion picture *The Empire Strikes Back*

What do a fish in a phone-book commercial, a writer talking about a baseball field in the middle of a farm in Iowa, and an evil character from a galaxy far, far away have in common? They have all come alive through the resonant baritone voice of the multitalented actor James Earl Jones.

Throughout his career James Earl Jones has performed in hundreds of film, television, and theater productions. From Broadway to Hollywood, as Shakespeare's Othello and Disney's Mufasa in *The Lion King*, his range as an actor has proved extraordinary. He has worked with some of the most talented performers to grace the stage and screen, including Jane Alexander, Alec Baldwin, Sean Connery, Kevin Costner, Colleen Dewhurst, Robert Duvall, Harrison Ford, Jodie Foster, Richard Harris, Al Pacino, Robert Redford, George C. Scott, Elizabeth Taylor, and Cicely Tyson.

Jones has received awards in almost every entertainment medium. He earned his first Best Actor Obie in 1962 for his performance in *Clandestine on the Morning Line* and additional Obies for *Baal* and *Othello* in 1965. (The Obie Awards, created by the magazine *Village Voice* in 1955, were created to publicly acknowledge and encourage the growing off-Broadway theater movement.) In 1969 Jones won a Tony Award—Broadway's highest honor—for his portrayal of Jack Johnson in the play *The Great White Hope*. (The Tony Award was established in 1947 in memory of Antoinette "Tony" Perry, a distinguished theater actor, director, and producer, and the chairman of the American Theatre Wing.) Eighteen years later he won another Best Actor Tony for his role in August Wilson's critically acclaimed play *Fences*.

Jones has also won other theatrical awards, including the Theatre World Award in 1962 for Most Promising Personality, with cowinners Robert Redford and Peter Fonda,

several Drama Desk Awards for theater work from 1964 to 1987, cable TV's Ace Award, a Grammy, a Best Actor and Hall of Fame Image Award from the National Association for the Advancement of Colored People, and several Golden Globe Awards. And in 1991, as a veteran of two television series, James Earl Jones was awarded a prestigious Best Actor Emmy from the Academy of Television Arts and Sciences for his performance in the drama series *Gabriel's Fire*. He received another for Best Supporting Actor in a Miniseries or Special for the Turner Network Television movie *Heat Wave*.

In 1992 James Earl Jones received perhaps one of the highest honors of his career, a National Medal of the Arts. The award is presented by the president of the United States to "individuals or groups who in the President's

Jones in costume for one of the many Broadway productions of Othello *in which he starred. Jones is shown here with Dianne Wiest as Desdemona.*

Flanked by First Lady Barbara Bush and President George Bush, Jones prepares to receive the 1992 National Medal of the Arts, one of the most prestigious awards of his long career.

judgment are deserving of special recognition by reason of their outstanding contributions to the excellence, growth, support and availability of the arts in the United States," and who offer inspiration to others through their achievements, support, or patronage. In addition to Jones, President George Bush presented medals to such notable Americans as opera singer Marilyn Horne, sculptor Allan Houser, performer Minnie Pearl, TV producer Robert Saudek, musicians Earl Scruggs and Billy Taylor, conductor Robert Shaw, film director Robert Wise, architects Robert Venturi and Denise Scott, and corporate patrons AT&T and Lila Wallace.

Though his theater, film, and television credits would be enough to fill out most careers, James Earl Jones's accomplishments go beyond acting and voice performances. He has loaned his voice to many narrative projects, including several documentaries and an audiotape of the New Testament. Many people recognize him from his appearances in over 30 commercial spots for Bell Atlantic telephone services, with whom he signed an exclusive contract in 1995.

To say that James Earl Jones's professional accomplishments are impressive would be an understatement. But what makes his achievements truly remarkable is the fact that he is a stutterer. In fact, from ages 6 to 14 he was virtually mute. Ironically, Jones is probably as recognizable by his voice as he is by his face. How can a stutterer be successful in a career that demands concise articulation of dialogue? As coauthor Penelope Niven writes of Jones in his autobiography, *Voices and Silences*:

> Because he is a stutterer, he shapes written and spoken language uniquely, and works with even more care than most writers do. His hands linger over every sentence. His eyes and ears are attuned to the resonance of words. And his years of silence have forged a sensitive listener and observer.

As a child, James Earl may have felt embarrassed and isolated by his problem, but he was not alone. Over 2.5 million people in the United States stutter. That's enough people to form a line from New York to California. For unknown reasons, stuttering affects men more than women: statistics show that 80 percent of adult stutterers are male. Most people begin stuttering between the ages of two and six, during the time they are developing the skills to form verbal sounds and to speak words (James Earl began stuttering at age four). Of two- and three-year-olds, an equal number of boys and girls stutter. The same study found that girls actually begin stuttering earlier than boys but are more likely to outgrow it.

What is stuttering? Simply defined, it happens when words are not spoken smoothly. These abnormal breaks in

All speech sounds are formed by blowing air from the lungs through the trachea over the vocal cords, which are located in the larynx. When the cords lie flat no sound is created, but when they are stretched out the passing air makes them vibrate. The air then passes through the epiglottis and into the mouth. No one knows exactly what causes stuttering, and causes may vary from person to person. However, tension in neck and facial muscles may affect one's speech, and for this reason many stutterers have more difficulty when they are tired, nervous, excited, or upset.

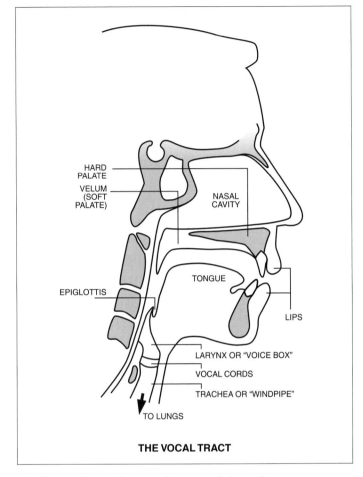

HARD
PALATE

VELUM
(SOFT
PALATE)

NASAL
CAVITY

TONGUE

EPIGLOTTIS

LIPS

LARYNX OR "VOICE BOX"

VOCAL CORDS

TRACHEA OR "WINDPIPE"

TO LUNGS

THE VOCAL TRACT

the flow of speech can take any of three forms: stoppage (no sound at all), repetitions of letters (for example, "st-st-st-station"), or prolongations of sounds and syllables (such as "ccccccaaaan't"). In some cases stuttering may be accompanied by unusual facial and body movements, like blinking, trembling of the lips, gasping, jerking of the head, and contortions of the body.

No one really knows what causes stuttering. Although no one stutters all the time, everyone stutters occasionally. In fact, a small percentage of speech flow interruptions are quite normal in both adults and children. For children, some stuttering is part of speech and language development. Adults often hesitate while speaking, interjecting words like "uh" or "um." However, chronic stutterers do so more often than most people and in specific situations, such as when they are excited, nervous, or tired. Some have more difficulty after awakening from a night's sleep; others stutter if they try to talk too quickly. And though emotional trauma does not cause stuttering, some people stutter when faced with talking with someone who intimidates them, like a boss or a teacher.

Because of the difficulty they have in communicating in a normal speech flow, stutterers take longer to express a thought, idea, or response. They describe feeling three types of sensations when stuttering occurs: a feeling of frustration because the words that they are trying to say just don't come out; muscle tension, usually in the jaw, lips, throat, and tongue; and emotional anxiety before, during, and after stuttering. Many stutterers also say that they feel as though they have "blanked out" or that their minds have gone "someplace else" during a stuttering episode. All of these factors make it difficult to correct stuttering problems.

Children have not yet learned appropriate adult behaviors, and they can react cruelly to stuttering. They may laugh at, tease, imitate, or otherwise embarrass the stutterer. This is particularly traumatic for child stutterers. Children don't want to be "different" or feel singled out. No one likes to be ridiculed, and many stutterers express feeling awkward or ashamed. As a result, they avoid communicating with others. As a boy James Earl Jones was so upset by the ridicule and teasing inflicted on him by other kids that he stopped talking and refused to attend Sunday worship services.

Although the causes of stuttering are unknown, there are treatments to help reduce or eliminate its occurrence. In his article "Stuttering—Frequently Asked Questions," author Thomas David Kehoe outlines several situations in which stuttering is less intense for most sufferers:

James Earl Jones displays his two 1991 Emmys for Best Lead Actor in a Drama Series in Gabriel's Fire *and Best Supporting Actor in a Miniseries or Special for* Heat Wave.

1. Speaking alone or to animals.
2. Speaking in chorus (in unison) with others.
3. Reading aloud.
4. Repeating a phrase.
5. Singing (because it requires measured speech and breathing).
6. Lowering the pitch of one's voice.

In overcoming his own stuttering problem, James Earl Jones used some of these techniques. In *Voices and Silences* he recalls that during the years when he was virtually silent, he did talk at times: "I talked to my family in basic terms; I talked to the farm animals; I talked to myself," he remembers. As Jones grew older, he discovered that his stutter disappeared when he recited poetry aloud. Memorizing lines of script dialogue also requires repetition and seemed easier than normal speech. We might think that speaking in public would be frightening for a stutterer, but an acting career actually allows the stutterer to improve his or her speech using some of the methods suggested above.

James Earl Jones has become one of the most sought-after voices in the entertainment industry. The years of his silence were painful, but rediscovering his voice inspired him: "I wanted to make up for the lost years when I did not speak," he said. "Eventually, inevitably, you yearn to lift your voice out of the silences and say, 'This is who I am.'"

To truly understand James Earl Jones's transformation from a mute child to the "voice of communication," one must journey back to his beginnings.

Exhausted workers pause during their labor in a Georgia cotton field. Decades after the Emancipation Proclamation officially ended slavery in the United States, many blacks, including James Earl Jones's family, still relied on farming for their livelihoods.

2

THOSE WHO CAME BEFORE

"Being myself is very complex, even as a racial entity. I am not only African, but I am Cherokee and Choctaw through my maternal grandmother. I am Irish through my maternal grandfather. . . . This rich, complicated heritage of blood does make for an interesting life, being fought over by so many different, wonderful ancestors."

—James Earl Jones, *Voices and Silences*

JAMES EARL JONES was born on January 17, 1931, in Arkabutla, Mississippi, a poor rural town in the soil-rich northwest Delta region of the state, not far from the Mississippi River. Most of its inhabitants lived off the land, raising fruits and vegetables, harvesting cotton, and sharecropping. In the 1930s, life was difficult for most blacks in the South. Not much had changed socially or economically in the 66 years since the Civil War had ended, and the lives of residents of Arkabutla were no exception.

By the time Abraham Lincoln was elected the 16th president of the United States on November 6, 1860, blacks had labored as slaves in

A group of Exodusters waits on a riverbank for a steamboat to carry them westward. Unlike Wyatt Connolly and his family, who remained in the South, many black southerners headed for Kansas and Oklahoma during Reconstruction in the hope of achieving greater economic independence.

America for over 250 years. During colonization, thousands of Africans were brought to America against their will and were bought and sold like property. Forced to work without pay for their owners, they had no civil rights, no possessions, and no freedom.

Although the Declaration of Independence proclaims the right to "Life, Liberty and the pursuit of Happiness," the United States Constitution, framed 11 years later in 1787, left the practice of slavery intact. As the country continued to grow and flourish, however, many Americans, particularly in the northern states, came to believe that slavery was "the deepest sin a society could commit." These men and women of the 19th century, who became known as abolitionists, not only freed their own slaves, but they also sought to have slavery abolished throughout the country. President Abraham Lincoln himself was a long-time opponent of slavery: as a congressman in 1849, he had proposed legislation that would have gradually freed all slaves. But in the South, where the agricultural workforce was predominantly slave labor, white plantation owners violently opposed such a plan.

More than 10 years later, when Lincoln ran for president, he campaigned with a promise to halt the expansion of slavery in America. This idea alarmed pro-slavery Southern whites even further, until South Carolina, Mississippi, Florida, Alabama, Georgia, Louisiana, Texas, Virginia, Arkansas, North Carolina, and Tennessee threatened to withdraw from the Union if Lincoln were elected president. He won the election, and South Carolina became the first state to secede on December 20, 1860. By the following June, 11 Southern states had withdrawn from the Union and had moved to establish their own nation, which they called the Confederate States of America. The United States was divided in two. On April 12, 1861, war broke out between the two factions when Confederate forces attacked Fort Sumter, a federal post in South Carolina. The fate of millions of enslaved blacks depended on the outcome of the conflict.

The Civil War, which lasted from 1861 to 1865, was the only war fought on American soil. The strife pitted state against state, countryman against countryman, and brother against brother and claimed more than 600,000 lives. More Americans died in this long, bloody war than in all other wars combined in U. S. history.

The war officially ended—and slavery was abolished— in 1865, after Confederate General Robert E. Lee surrendered to Union General Ulysses S. Grant at the Appomattox Courthouse in Virginia. The period following the war, 1866 to 1877, became known as Reconstruction, in which political, social, and economic wounds began to heal and the country rebuilt what had been destroyed in battle.

With the passage of the Fifteenth Amendment in 1870 black men gained the right to vote (no women of any race would be allowed to vote until 1920). Until 1872 a federal organization called the Freedman's Bureau gave former slaves educational opportunities by providing funds to open thousands of elementary schools and to teach blacks to read. The bureau also provided food, health care, and legal assistance. Under the Civil Rights Act of 1875 Congress forbade racial segregation in transportation, hotels, theaters, and other public places. Hundreds of new churches were established where blacks could worship freely. These churches would become vital in black communities, for they were places to meet, teach, learn, and exchange ideas.

During Reconstruction, however, the economic conditions of most blacks did not improve and, in many cases, even deteriorated. No longer supported financially by slave owners, blacks needed to find other ways to survive. The federal government failed to provide sufficient economic aid, and many Southern blacks were compelled to move to the more industrialized North in the hope of finding better jobs. For those who remained in the South, land ownership provided the best chance for economic advancement because the region's economy was still predominantly based on agriculture. Having acquired few other skills, many southern blacks continued working at what they knew best—harvesting cotton and other crops. The great difference was that they were now free men and women who were paid for their labor.

If the abolishment of slavery brought the hope of legal and economic equality to blacks, the end of Reconstruction signaled social hardship and despair. As the 19th century waned, the attitudes ingrained in whites by slave owning were only intensified by the anger they felt over having "lost control" of blacks. In his book *The Community Builders*, Pierre Hauser describes the deepening racial hatred:

> The South's defeat in the Civil War, followed by Reconstruction, destroyed . . . slave society, but it could not eliminate the underlying social attitudes. Reconstruction, in fact, strengthened the desire of southern whites to hold blacks down, a desire intensified by the role blacks played in keeping former Confederates out of power during the first years after the war.

James Earl Jones's ancestors were among the blacks who stayed on in the South and began acquiring land. By the time James Earl was born his family owned several hundred acres of farmland in Arkabutla. But by then, the country was also in the grip of a fierce economic depression. When the New York stock market crashed on October 29th, 1929, America's economy spiraled downward. Thousands of businesses closed, banks failed, farms were abandoned, and mines and steel mills shut down. By 1931, over 12 million Americans were out of work. One in four whites lost his job; for blacks the figure was one out of two. Many families could no longer afford to buy necessities like food and clothing. Those who lived off the land could at least continue selling their crops. But in 1930 a drought hit the South, and raising enough food to feed one's own family became almost impossible.

Like James Earl Jones, American memoirist and poet Maya Angelou also grew up during the Great Depression.

Worried depositors mill around the locked and guarded doors of a bank in 1932. More than 10,000 banks failed during the Great Depression, wiping out the life savings of millions of Americans.

She lived in the small, poor, black town of Stamps, Arkansas, where most residents farmed for a living. In her critically acclaimed autobiography, *I Know Why the Caged Bird Sings*, Angelou describes the effects of the economic collapse on African Americans:

> I think that everyone thought that the Depression, like everything else, was for the whitefolks, so it had nothing to do with them. Our people had lived off the land and counted on cotton-picking and hoeing and chopping seasons to bring in the cash needed to buy shoes, clothes, books, and light farm equipment. It was when the owners of cotton fields dropped the payment of ten cents for a pound of cotton to eight, seven and finally five that the Negro community realized that the Depression, at least, did not discriminate.

James Earl Jones came into the world on the land his family had owned since Reconstruction. His great-great-grandfather, Brice, was kidnapped from Africa as a boy and sold to a Mississippi plantation owner around 1820. Brice worked as a slave in the cotton fields for the next 35 or 40 years, during which he met an Irish servant named Parthenia Connolly, who worked on the same plantation. Parthenia was an indentured servant, a person who agreed to work for a period of time (usually five to seven years) without receiving wages in order to repay the cost of being brought to America. An employer of an indentured servant usually provided food, clothing, and shelter to the servant until the term of the agreement was fulfilled. Then the servant was free to leave.

Brice and Parthenia fell in love, and when Parthenia finished her term of service, they married. It was quite remarkable that these two were allowed to create a family and share a life together, since Brice was a black slave and Parthenia was a free white woman. Secretly Parthenia taught Brice how to read and write. Years later, having learned that education is true liberation, they would instill its importance in their children.

When the Civil War ended and Brice was finally a free man, he was in need of a last name (slaves were given the last names of their white owners to signify that they were their property). He took Parthenia's, and Connolly became the family name. The Connollys had nine children in all; their third child, Wyatt, would become the great-grandfather of James Earl.

It was Wyatt who began buying cheap land in Tate County, Mississippi, acquiring more than 300 acres in all. One can only imagine what it was like for him to hold in his hands the deed to his own land when only a few years earlier he had been legally forbidden to buy or own property.

Wyatt read widely to learn about cultivating the soil so that it would yield as much produce as possible. Acre by acre, seed by seed, in soil that was believed to be unfit for growing food, Wyatt eventually raised enough crops for his family to eat and to sell at market. He married Sharlett Jeter, who was of mixed African and Native American blood, and built a home in the middle of his farmland, which he called the "Home House." Six sons and five daughters were born in the Home House: Ed, James Carver, John Henry, Esseck, Ira, Nimrod, Mary, Lillian, Sidney, Lenna, and Eliza. As they grew up, each of the children settled in the community surrounding the homestead. James Earl Jones described the strong family ties of his ancestors and the importance of the land Wyatt had purchased:

> Wyatt and Sharlett Jeter Connolly's Home House sheltered their children and grandchildren, and stood staunch at the center of the little universe of acres and family and heritage they created in Tate County, Mississippi. The houses their children built radiated from that hub, tied to it by the spokes of land Wyatt parceled out to his sons and taught them to farm. . . . The land made that possible, the land was sanctuary and security, the land was the pathway to the future. The land was home.

Wyatt also built a Methodist church school on his

Although she was eccentric and temperamental, James Earl's grandmother Maggie Connolly (or "Mama") was also a deeply spiritual woman who loved the energy and enthusiasm of the Baptist services she attended. Much like the southern worshipers shown here, Mama often became carried away by spirited sermons and lively gospel music.

land, and on Sundays the children and grandchildren gathered there to worship and eat dinner together. Wyatt had acquired a modest collection of books and encouraged everyone in his family to read them. All of the children memorized Bible verses and recited them at dinner. As his parents had in the days following Reconstruction, Wyatt believed that spiritual and intellectual growth were essential.

Wyatt allotted 40 acres of his own land to each of his six sons, which they had to earn and pay for. The third of Wyatt and Sharlett's children, John Henry, would become James Earl's grandfather, and on his share of his father's land John Henry built a four-room house. As he had with his other sons, Wyatt taught John Henry how to be a successful farmer, how to manage a farm, plant the crops, milk the cows, and slaughter the animals. He also taught them hunting and carpentry. Not long after, John Henry married Maggie Anderson, an independent, moody woman who was part black, part Choctaw Indian.

Nothing gave John Henry more pleasure than seeing his children eat well. He was a quiet, hardworking man who usually worked alone. But there were also stories about him leading a double life that included a second wife and family in another part of Mississippi. There was even talk about a secret career, in which John Henry and a white freight yard switchman conspired to overturn freight cars carrying produce and sell the damaged fruits and vegetables at half price in black neighborhoods. Whether or not these tales of improprieties were true, John Henry never neglected his responsibilities to his family or to the farm.

In contrast to her husband, Maggie Anderson Connolly, by accounts from her own kin, was a strong-willed woman who had plenty to say about most subjects and never hesitated to express them to whomever would listen. She was a complex woman with a zest for adventure and a touch of wanderlust, and she was so unusual that some members of her family believed that she had the power to cast spells. An avid reader, Maggie filled her shelves with books about mysticism, the occult, yoga, and Eastern philosophy. Her views were as unorthodox as she was eccentric. Though fiercely independent, she had a strong nurturing and protective nature where home and family were concerned. She was also deeply distrustful of whites and remained wary of them throughout her life.

But Maggie also had a softer, more spiritual side. She loved music and had a passion for God, and she worshipped in church with electric energy and enthusiasm. When she felt the power of the Spirit, she'd speak in tongues and raise her hands up, shouting, "Hallelujah!" over and over until exhaustion overcame her. Maggie also had a gift for storytelling and spun dramatic yarns of magic and horror. In Arkabutla, where there were no televisions and few people owned or read books, telling stories was a form of entertainment.

Maggie and John Henry followed the Connolly tradition of raising large families and had 11 children—seven daughters and four sons—all born in the house that John Henry built. Two of the children, Ruby and Wesley, did not survive childhood. The remaining nine children were Ruth, Bessie, Anna Bell, Thelma, Ozella, Helen, Henry Lee (or H. L.), Hubert Berkely (or H. B.), and Randy. The eldest daughter, Ruth, would give birth to James Earl seven months before her 21st birthday.

Thirty-one of James Earl Jones's relatives are descendants of Brice and Parthenia Connolly. Twenty-two of them—including James Earl himself—were born on the family land. The deep-rooted commitment to family and home, the work ethic, and the self-reliance that had been forged from the beliefs of Parthenia and Brice would be instilled in James Earl, as they had been in all those who came before.

During the early years of this century, many southern blacks—including Jones's great-grandfather Wyatt—founded church schools to insure that their children would receive formal educations. This photograph illustrates a typical one-room building that functioned as both church and school.

3

"QUESTIONS NOT ASKED, WORDS NOT SPOKEN"

"One of the hardest things in life is having words in your heart that you can't utter."

—James Earl Jones, *Voices and Silences*

JAMES EARL JONES'S mother, Ruth, was born on August 24, 1910, the second child of Maggie and John Henry. Ruth's childhood was hard. "Papa," as John Henry was called, moved the family often in search of work, better schools, and bigger places to live. They lived in Tennessee; in Missouri, where Papa worked at a steel mill in St. Louis; in Detroit, Michigan; then in Gary, Indiana, where Papa found a job at another steel mill. When he could not find work elsewhere, Papa moved everybody back to the Home House to raise crops. Even during the most difficult times, the farm provided food for the family. They could always count on the homestead and the Home House to sustain them.

Papa wanted his children to have good educations, but because there were only four high schools open to blacks in Mississippi, schooling opportunities were rare. In addition, the older Connolly children could

33

only attend classes about four months out of the year because they were needed on the farm or at the nearby steel mill during the rest of the year. Many years later, when Ruth was about 75 years old, her sister Ozella asked her to write about her early life. Among her recollections of the family's constant settling down and pulling up stakes was this reflection about education:

> The saddest part of it all [trying to get an education] was the school system for black children. . . . Pa made a couple of attempts to get the kids in a better school [but c]ould [not] board that many out. One fall he rented a house in Memphis. We all moved in to go [to school] in the city which was good. But with no other livelihood than farming it was hard. Pa was back on the farm trying to get things going. One or two years the oldest stayed in Memphis some and went to school there with kin.

Though Ruth did not have the opportunity to continue her own studies, she did stay involved in education, becoming a teacher at the Home House church that her grandfather Wyatt built. Wyatt knew that the state of Mississippi would not fund a school building for black children, but he guessed that once such a school was open with pupils in attendance, the county would be forced to hire a teacher. Ruth was a popular teacher among the younger children, including her own brothers and sisters. She was also an accomplished seamstress and made costumes for the students to wear in the pageants that she wrote and directed.

But Ruth had a dark side too. She often brooded and would become moody and withdrawn without warning. One day she simply stopped teaching at the church school and went to Memphis, Tennessee, where she took a job as a maid. The habit of moving from one place to another, which Ruth had learned as a child, would stay with her for most of her life. Like John Henry, she drifted from place to place, from job to job, settling down wherever she found work: as a migrant worker in the Delta, a domestic

Robert Earl Jones in a portrait taken by Carl Van Vechten while Jones was performing in Langston Hughes's play Don't You Want to be Free? *James Earl Jones was 18 years old before he spoke with his father; he did not meet him until three years later.*

in Memphis, a tailor and seamstress in the Midwest. But just as John Henry did, she would always return to the family farm. On one of those visits home, in the summer of 1929, she attended a church picnic in Coldwater, a small town near Arkabutla. There she met Robert Earl Jones, James Earl's father.

Despite having been frequently uprooted, Ruth's family was stable. Papa and Mama stayed together to raise their kids and to cope with life in the economically

John Henry (or "Papa") assigned farming chores, such as the plowing shown here, to each member of his large family. James Earl was still very young when he was given his first chores: milking cows, gathering eggs, and helping to harvest the fields.

South. Robert Earl Jones was not as fortunate, however. Though the day-to-day lives of Ruth and Robert Earl were not so different, their families were. Robert Earl was an only child. His parents, Elnora and Robert, separated when Robert Earl was about 13. The boy was left to work the farm that his family had leased and to look after his mother. His father, a self-ordained preacher and the grandson of slaves, left Coldwater. Robert Earl saw very little of him after that.

As Robert Earl got older and began to look more like his father, Elnora wanted less to do with her son. Looking for the love and support of family, Robert Earl eventually went to Arkabutla to visit his father. But their meeting went badly and he returned to Coldwater soon after. Though he remained with his mother, Robert Earl received little of the warmth and affection that children seek from their parents.

In 1929 Robert Earl convinced Elnora to give up the farm, and mother and son moved to Memphis. There Robert Earl took various odd jobs while Elnora worked as a maid. Robert Earl had become quite strong and athletic, and he took up boxing. Soon he was good enough to compete, using "Battling Bill Stovall" as his professional name. But though he had some success as a Golden Gloves boxer, he fought mostly for the money and the attention. His heart was not really in it.

When Robert Earl met Ruth at the church picnic he was immediately attracted to her. She was beautiful and smart. She told him that she had completed the sixth grade and that she had taught at her grandfather's church school. Robert Earl himself had only managed to complete the third grade. Ruth liked Robert Earl too, and they began dating soon after they met. In the early spring of 1930 they married and moved to Memphis, where both took jobs with a wealthy white family—Ruth as a maid and Robert Earl as a butler and chauffeur. The family allowed them to live rent-free in a garage apartment on the estate grounds. The Great Depression of 1929 had put millions of Americans, especially blacks, out of work. They were fortunate to have jobs.

The couple was happy for a while, but Ruth was constantly moody. Moreover, Maggie and John Henry Connolly hadn't approved of their daughter's choice of husband. When Maggie finally decided to visit them in Memphis, she criticized their apartment and the way they were living. Because Ruth took her mother's words to heart and did not defend her husband, Robert Earl began to feel like a failure.

Ruth and Robert Earl's marriage lasted less than a year.

Not long after Maggie's visit, Ruth, now 20 and pregnant, left Robert Earl and moved home to have her baby. In the early morning hours of January 17, 1931, she went into labor. Maggie sent for the same midwife who had helped her deliver all of her own children. At 6:05 a.m., in the same house where she had been born, Ruth gave birth to her only child. She named him James Earl.

James Earl's father would visit his son only once. In *Voices and Silences*, James Earl tells the story of his early childhood as it was told to him:

> Robert Earl stayed on in Memphis for a time after I was born, boxing, working at odd jobs, feeling his guilt about the marriage, and believing himself a failure as a man, a husband, and now, a father. He and my aunts have told me that some of the family persuaded Ruth and Maggie to allow Robert Earl to see me when I was an infant. He came, and pulled back the netting from my carriage—and I looked into his face. He lifted me up and I squalled. I was a baby. He was a stranger to me. He took it as a personal affront, and left, and we never saw each other again until I was twenty-one.

While growing up, James Earl had less difficulty with the fact that his father wasn't around than he did with his mother's continual comings and goings. He didn't know his father, didn't spend time with him, and never expected to see him. But Ruth continued to wander, leaving her son in his grandparents' care and coming home periodically. The times apart from his mother were painful, but James Earl felt anguish even during her brief visits, anticipating the time when she would leave him again. Sometimes he would go to her, visiting her wherever she was, especially in Memphis. But the visits were short, and he still felt great distress and confusion when he left for home. Why was his mother away so often? Why did she send him back to the farm when he came to visit her? Why didn't Ruth come home to stay?

Jones remembered hearing an argument one night

between Ruth and Maggie. Ruth wanted to take James Earl with her to the Delta, and Maggie was dead set against the idea. Eventually Maggie wore Ruth down, and she agreed to leave her son in his grandparents' care. John Henry, Maggie, and all of James Earl's aunts and uncles became his "mothers and fathers."

As a toddler James Earl followed John Henry everywhere, and he learned a great deal about life on a farm. Papa took pride in the fact that he was able to feed and take care of his large family. James Earl watched John Henry feed the chickens, till the soil, and plant the crops. Eventually the boy would be assigned his own chores too, such as milking the cows, making butter, gathering eggs from the hens, and harvesting the fields.

John Henry Connolly was essentially James Earl's father, not his grandparent. He refused to shield James Earl from life's realities. Once, for example, one of the farm sows was giving birth to a litter of piglets when one became lodged in the sow's birth canal. John Henry waited with James Earl to see whether the piglet would work its way out on its own. When he realized that it had died, he reached in and pulled out the animal to save its mother. Similarly, John Henry didn't keep James Earl from witnessing livestock being slaughtered for food. Farm life connected one not only to peacefulness and beauty, John Henry believed, but to harsh realities as well.

Papa acted as James Earl's father in other ways too. He would take him fishing at Lost Lake, a swampy pond not far from the farm. Although he did so with all the boys, he took each one separately, for these outings were not meant for catching fish so much as they were to spend time alone with each of his children. Papa wasn't much for asking whether the children needed to talk or for wondering whether something was on their minds. Going fishing was his way of making himself available to each child in private. If something was troubling them, the boys knew, this was when they could share their worries with Papa.

John Henry and Maggie gave James Earl the security and sense of family that he did not receive from his parents. The other stable force in his life was the Home House itself and the land that his family owned. He could wander Papa's farm or roam freely over acres of land and feel comfortable and familiar with his surroundings in a world that was anything but secure. Although he didn't have toys like other kids, he could explore the boundaries of the land, observe the many "critters" that lived in the area creeks and mud holes, and invent imaginary games. He was unaware that the future of the homestead was in jeopardy.

Papa and Mama had talked about moving north for some time. Finding better educational opportunities for his children was always in John Henry's thoughts. He talked often with Maggie about moving the family to a place where the children could get better schooling. Though it was too late for Ruth, Bessie, H. L., and H. B., who were past high school age, John Henry and Maggie were determined to improve the educational opportunities of their youngest children. Aside from their own five children still living at home, they were also raising James Earl and Bessie's son, Robert Earl, who was a few years younger than his cousin.

The Connollys' hopes for a better life were far from unique. Only 20 years earlier, a wave of southern blacks had begun heading north in search of the same. Their journeys together came to be known as the Great Migration. Leaving behind the hatred and bigotry of southern whites who were bitter over their defeat in the Civil War, blacks dared to hope that life in the North would bring them a renewed sense of place and self-respect.

Between 1910 and 1930, more than one million blacks moved from the predominantly rural South to the more industrialized North. The national economy had been stimulated by the outbreak of World War I, and factories that produced military equipment increased their productivity. Employers searched for workers to fill positions left

vacant by those who had gone to war.

Before this time John Henry had frequently traveled north for work, but he had always returned to Tate County, to Arkabutla, and to the Home House. Now he would no longer leave and return as opportunities arose. He decided to sell his beloved 40 acres, on which the Home House was situated, and move the family north for good. It was not an easy decision, nor one that he and Maggie came to quickly. After much thought and discussion, Papa felt that moving out of the South was the only way to do better for himself and his family. For her part, Mama was certain that the North held better husbands for her daughters and that the move would satisfy her hunger for adventure. She was weary of the powerful racism she experienced in Mississippi and longed to leave it behind.

The Connollys were among the many black southern families who left their homes for the long journey north during the period known as the Great Migration.

And so, like thousands of other blacks, the Connollys left the South to begin a new life in a new place.

Before the move, John Henry bought 40 acres of land, sight unseen, in what he was told was a suburb of Grand Rapids, Michigan. He and H. B. planned to drive there first and get settled, then send for the rest of the family, who would travel by train. For the children, the move seemed sudden—and frightening. One day, without any discussion, John Henry and H. B. loaded the family car with luggage and placed a mattress in the backseat so that they could stop and sleep during the long drive without the expense of stopping at hotels. When they were finished packing, Papa called to James Earl to get in the car.

Thinking that he was leaving for Michigan with Papa and H. B., James Earl climbed in. They drove for a while before pulling up in front of a nice house with a picket fence. Waiting at the front door of the house was a smiling woman—Elnora Jones, James Earl's paternal grandmother.

But they were in Memphis, not Grand Rapids. Papa told him this would be his new home. The smiling woman was a stranger to James Earl; he could not understand why Papa and Mama would want to leave him behind. He refused to get out of the car and clutched the mattress with all his strength. Finally, after exchanging a few words with Elnora, Papa gave in and got back in the car. He drove back to Arkabutla to drop off James Earl before heading to Michigan. The shock of this event would stay with the young boy for years, as James Earl remembered in his memoir:

> I stayed with Mama and the aunts and uncles [in Mississippi] until it was time to take the train to Michigan. But everything had changed for me, the safety of home, the sense of belonging in the family. Even before we moved to Michigan, a world ended for me, the safe world of childhood.
>
> There are questions not asked, words not spoken. I could not talk to Papa and Mama about their decision to leave

me behind in Memphis, and then their reprieve. There was so much I could not ask or say. The move from Mississippi to Michigan was supposed to be a glorious event. For me it was a heartbreak.

All that he had known, all that had been safe and familiar, was now gone. Soon after the family arrived in Michigan, James Earl began to stutter.

Although in America tobacco is traditionally grown almost exclusively in the Southeast, John Henry was determined to continue raising the crop after he moved his family to Michigan. His tobacco farm in Dublin probably resembled this homestead.

4

THE SONG
OF HIAWATHA

"A nonverbal person beginning to speak is not unlike an illiterate person beginning to read: what captures the imagination is not the twisting and turning of ideas, but the flooding of feeling. I discovered that graceful language was fluid with sounds. Passion graces itself."

—James Earl Jones, *Voices and Silences*

WHEN PAPA AND H. B. got to Michigan, they discovered that the land Papa had purchased on trust was not in a suburb of Grand Rapids after all. Instead, the farmland that John Henry bought was in Dublin, Manistee County, about 100 miles north of Grand Rapids. Although the property was similar in size to his Arkabutla homestead, the soil was thin and sandy, not nearly as suitable for farming. Nevertheless, Papa and H. B. believed that it had possibilities: they had been surprised to discover that the property, touted as "improved," had a chicken house.

When Papa sent word back to Maggie that the main building on their new land was a chicken house, however, he stirred up quite a bit of talk. To those living in Arkabutla, such a structure was a small, flim-

Until they began attending high school, James Earl Jones and his uncle Randy attended a one-room schoolhouse similar to the one shown here.

sy enclosure surrounded by fencing to keep the chickens from wandering away. But the one in Dublin was nothing of the sort. Long, sturdy, and wooden, with a concrete floor, this chicken house was no makeshift structure. It had been constructed as the main building of a thriving poultry business and had been solidly built to endure the harsh Michigan winters. Papa and H. B. worked on preparing the chicken house to live in. When it was ready, he sent word to Maggie to bring the rest of the family.

When one is five years old, time and distance have no

meaning. Where was Michigan, anyway? What did it look like? Was the trip there as long as the one to Elnora's house in Memphis? All young James Earl knew was that the family was moving, leaving behind the Home House and their other relatives. The only memory Jones has of the trip is of playing "peekaboo" games on the train with his cousin Robert Earl and a stranger who was also making the trip north.

That first winter in Dublin, Papa spent most of his time working on the other structures on the property. He made use of all the materials left scattered around by the previous owner. There was a farmhouse that had never been completed, and he disassembled it to use the timber and boards on the chicken house. He used the hay barn to stable a horse and another long chicken barn to shelter the cows and other farm animals during the winter. Finding a pile of railroad cross ties on the property, he used some of them to build a storm shelter to store potatoes and other vegetables in a cool place when the weather got warmer, and he saved the rest for firewood.

Shortly after the Connollys settled in their new home, James Earl and his uncle Randy, who was only four years older than Jones, began attending elementary school in a little schoolhouse in Dublin. Classes for all eight grades were held in a one-room building. Because everyone was together in one room, each student was exposed to a variety of subjects at several levels.

On the first day of school, James Earl and Randy thought that everyone else spoke strangely. Even the other black children sounded different to them. Up north, people rolled their *r*s. Here, the kids called Jones "James Earrrrl," not "James Uhl," as his name had been pronounced in the South. Though the two boys laughed about this with each other, they didn't do so around the other children.

Randy had begun stuttering while the family was still living in Arkabutla, and James Earl teased him terribly. But by the time the family arrived in Michigan, he too was stuttering quite badly. Feeling self-conscious—and certain that he was cursed for poking fun at Randy—James Earl retreated into silence. He spoke little; in fact, from the time the family moved north until he was 14 years old, he was virtually mute.

On a farm, people raise their voices all the time: to call the cows and pigs, for example. The family tolerated James's silence, but Papa missed hearing his grandson's voice. As an adult, James Earl would wonder whether part of the reason he withdrew into silence was because, in his mind, he thought he needed to remain in the background causing no trouble so he would be allowed to stay with the family. He had never asked John Henry or Maggie why they had originally planned to leave him with his paternal grandmother, Elnora, before moving to Michigan.

In school Jones's teachers never pressured him to speak in class. Instead, they assessed his learning through written exercises and exams. And though the kids at school didn't laugh at him, the kids at church did. Like his father before him, Papa had decided to establish his own church when he couldn't find a suitable place in Manistee for Sunday worship services. In the very house of worship that John Henry built, James Earl was forced to stand before the congregation and recite his Sunday school verses. Most of the children laughed at his speech and thought he was funny. Although in later life Jones would understand that these children weren't intentionally mean-spirited, he felt humiliated at the time. In an interview for the television series *A&E Biography*, Jones discussed the feelings that a stutterer experiences:

> I want to be politically incorrect for a moment and say that stutterers are funny as hell. And anybody that makes fun of 'em or inadvertently laughs, I understand it completely, as a stutterer. It's not that I condone ridicule, but I knew why the kids were laughing at me, behind me, in Sunday school. It's so nervous-making, it creates such anxiety in everybody, that you laugh.

James Earl's church experiences were so mortifying that one day when he was about eight years old, he made a decision that he kept into adulthood: he would not go to church anymore. Although John Henry and Maggie were very religious and were unhappy with the boy's decision, they allowed James Earl to stay home.

Even though racist attitudes were often stronger in the South, James Earl surprisingly did not recall experiencing such treatment until the family moved to Michigan. On the train north, he discovered that blacks were not allowed to eat in the dining car with whites. Maggie had to pack sandwiches, and they ate in the passenger car whenever they were hungry. One day in Michigan, all the schoolchildren were gathered together to visit the dentist—but the whites

After the Plessy v. Ferguson *decision of 1896, in which the Supreme Court ruled against a black man named Homer Adolph Plessy who refused to sit in the "colored" section of a train in Louisiana, the "separate but equal" policy allowed the passage of thousands of discriminatory state laws. Perhaps because he was very young at the time, James Earl Jones did not recall experiencing discrimination until his family moved north and he began attending school.*

were loaded into one car and the blacks into another. James Earl was shocked; Maggie was furious; but John Henry was simply matter-of-fact about it. Some things didn't change no matter where you lived, he discovered.

Living on a farm in Michigan was very different from life in Mississippi. For one thing, the growing season was much shorter in the North, so it was more difficult to make a profit by farming. Still, John Henry followed the ways of his father, Wyatt, and read everything he could find about growing crops in the northern climate. He read the *Farmer's Almanac*, studied agricultural journals, and even tried to grow some of the same crops he had in Arkabutla, including tobacco and peanuts. Others were skeptical; many people told him that he would never get tobacco to grow there, but he kept trying until the crop began to thrive.

America entered World War II in December 1941, after Japanese forces attacked the U.S. Pacific Fleet in Pearl Harbor, Hawaii (facing page). Unlike most Americans, Maggie Connolly was a Communist sympathizer and listened avidly to pro-Japanese propaganda radio programs broadcast by several women known collectively as Tokyo Rose. Shown here is Iva Toguri D'Aquino (left), one of the women who were convicted of treason for these wartime broadcasts.

Papa expected everybody to work the farm. He called the kids his "field hands." In return they called him the "straw boss" (one who supervises other workers while performing his own duties). In addition to tobacco and peanuts they also raised melons, potatoes, cabbage, and cucumbers. In the neighboring small town of Wellstone there was a brine factory, and the Connolly clan sold their cucumber crop there to be made into pickles.

As always, in good times or bad, the Connollys relied on farming for their own food as well. It had sustained them for several years when the country was in the throes of the Great Depression. Now the United States would encounter an even greater struggle—World War II.

The events leading to the war started in Europe in the mid-1930s. After the death of German president Paul von

Hindenburg in 1934, a fanatical Nationalist named Adolf Hitler appointed himself the *führer*, or leader, of the country. Hitler had a grand and horrible vision of a German empire that would control all of Europe—and "cleanse" itself of all "inferior" races. At the same time, in western Europe, Benito Mussolini, the premier of Italy, had established a Fascist government—one that stressed nation and race above all else—and had also set out to claim more land for himself. And in the South Pacific, Japan, under the leadership of Emperor Hirohito, conquered island after island while battling with China at home. These powerful and dangerous men—Hitler, Mussolini, and Hirohito—eventually formed an alliance that was called the Axis Powers, with the ultimate goal of ruling the globe.

In the Soviet Union, meanwhile, another dictator was in power. Joseph Stalin, an ardent Communist from the days of the Russian Revolution, ruled Russia with an iron fist for more than 25 years. Hitler knew that he could not conquer Europe while waging war with the Soviet Union, so in August 1939, after an all-night conference between the two leaders, Hitler and Stalin signed a public pact of nonaggression. What the rest of the world did not know was that they had also agreed to divide eastern Europe between them. Germany would take western Poland and the Soviet Union would take eastern Poland and the Baltic states of Estonia, Latvia, and Lithuania.

On September 1, 1939, Hitler attacked Poland. Two days later Great Britain and France declared war on Germany, launching World War II. The United States entered the war two years later, when Japan attacked the U.S. Pacific Fleet at Pearl Harbor in Hawaii.

Ironically, the war proved good for the American economy. At the conclusion of World War I, the United States had reduced the size and strength of its military forces. Rebuilding these resources quickly was paramount now that the country was once again at war. Thousands of jobs were created as factories stepped up production and the demand for military equipment—planes, tanks, guns, and ammunition—soared.

Like most American families, the Connollys sat by the radio nightly to hear the reports of each day's battles. Although most Americans strongly supported U.S. involvement in the war, a few felt that democracy as the United States practiced it was unsuccessful, and therefore sympathized with the Fascist, Communist, and imperialist dictators.

Maggie Connolly was one of them. She had been pro-Soviet for some years and liked what she had heard about the principles of Communism. During the war, she listened to "Tokyo Rose" radio broadcasts (a nickname given by U.S. troops in the Pacific to several women who broadcast enemy propaganda during the war). Often these broadcasts would launch appeals to American blacks, urging them toward solidarity with people of color worldwide. In Mama's thinking, that meant that Asian people were much like blacks. Feeling a sense of kinship with the Japanese, Maggie aligned herself with Hirohito and Hitler. How bad could Hitler be, she reasoned, if he was an ally of an Asian country? As far as Mama was concerned, Hitler could bomb Mississippi!

The war touched the Connolly home directly when Ozella's husband, Bob, left home to fight in the Pacific campaign. Every day, Ozella prayed for Bob's safe return and listened with particular interest to news about the fighting in that part of the world. But Mama still believed steadfastly in America's war enemies. On the day that the aircraft named *Enola Gay* dropped an atomic bomb on Hiroshima, Japan, virtually ending the war, Mama turned to Ozella and said, "Don't think it's over. Tojo [the Japanese general] will win yet."

If Mama was eccentric when James Earl was a toddler, she had grown even more so by the time he was a teenager. Jones himself believed that she may have been afflicted by mental illness. "Before her life was over, Mama was

James Earl was still a silent student when he began attending Dickson High (shown here in a photo from the 1930s). Only after Donald Crouch (facing page, in 1981) encouraged Jones to read and write poetry did the young student begin to speak again.

surely touched with madness," he relates in his autobiography. "She wasn't deranged—she was just strangely arranged."

In the fall of 1945 Jones enrolled in Dickson High School in Brethren, Michigan. It was quite a change to go from the one-room schoolhouse in Dublin to a two-story brick building with 10 full-time teachers on staff. Though he still spoke little and kept mostly to himself, he enjoyed his classes and the many extracurricular activities offered. He was an A student and a member of the varsity basketball and track teams.

Although Jones had matured into a young man, his mother Ruth's absences still caused him great pain. She had married again and moved to St. Louis, Missouri, not long after the Connolly clan had arrived in Michigan. Ruth still took jobs as a seamstress wherever she could find work and still came to Michigan for annual summer visits.

Meanwhile, James Earl's father, Robert Earl, had moved to New York in the 1930s after being cast as the sparring partner of the famous boxer Joe Louis in the film *The Spirit of Youth*. Acting had seemed to be an easier way to earn a living than boxing, and Robert Earl began looking for theater jobs. He arrived in New York shortly after the Harlem Renaissance, when many black artists, writers, and actors were achieving great success in their fields. Working in the theater, he met such notable figures as actor Paul Robeson and writer Langston Hughes.

Around the time Jones turned 14 he received a letter from his father, in which was enclosed a train ticket to New York. Unfortunately Maggie and John Henry, who had never allowed James Earl to have contact with his father, forbade the boy to accept Robert Earl's invitation. It would be several years before James Earl would have another opportunity to meet his father; by then, his life would have changed drastically.

In school Jones was exposed to a wide variety of subjects. He loved science, partly because it reminded him of science fiction, a world of fantasy and adventure. He especially liked reading the works of Jules Verne, a French writer whose novels included *A Journey to the Center of the Earth*, *Around the World in 80 Days*, and *20,000 Leagues under the Sea*. He was beginning to learn about great literature, and this knowledge opened up a new world that he had not known in Mississippi.

One teacher played a pivotal role in Jones's life—Donald Crouch, a retired college professor who took a job at Dickson High teaching English, Latin, and history. His literary assignments included reading classics like those by

William Shakespeare, Ralph Waldo Emerson, and Henry Wadsworth Longfellow. Jones especially loved Longfellow's long poem *The Song of Hiawatha*. He liked the fact that Longfellow had written the poem about the Chippewa Indians, who had once occupied the region around Lake Superior in Michigan:

> By the shore of Gitche Gumee,
> By the shining Big-Sea-Water,
> At the doorway of his wigwam,
> In the pleasant Summer morning,
> Hiawatha stood and waited.
> All the air was full of freshness,
> All the earth was bright and joyous,
> And before him, through the sunshine,
> Westward toward the neighboring forest,
> Passed in golden swarms the Ahmo,
> Passed the bees, the honey-makers,
> Burning, singing in the sunshine. . . .

Soon James Earl was not simply reading poetry; he also began writing his own. The taste of a Florida grapefruit was the inspiration for one such poem. Proud of his "Ode to a Grapefruit," Jones turned in the poem to fulfill a writing assignment.

Crouch saw the intelligence and talent hidden behind the teenager's silence and suspected that there was more to it than shyness. Although he had never before forced Jones to speak publicly, he now asked Jones to recite his poem aloud before his classmates. Jones nervously stood up in front of the class, expecting to stutter and to feel embarrassed. Instead the words flowed fluently and smoothly. To his amazement, he did not stutter.

What Jones didn't know at the time was that speaking in a poetic rhythm is easier for a stutterer than using regular speech. Reading and writing poetry would be the key to unlocking his silence. With this new discovery, Crouch realized that they could use recitation to help Jones speak again. Jones later described his exhilaration:

I would have glorious experiences reading Edgar Allan Poe aloud. I could throw back the curtains in the high school gymnasium, step out on the stage with a lighted candle, and read Edgar Allan Poe—and everybody would *listen*. Those were special nights for me.

An orator was born.

James Earl Jones as a young actor.

5

A VOICE
NOW HEARD

"Even though I'd had some acting courses at the university, I didn't consider myself an actor; but I wanted to be in the theatre, so the hammer [working behind the scenes] was the first thing."

—James Earl Jones, *With a Strong Voice*
(*A&E Biography* series)

ONCE JONES BEGAN to talk, it seemed he couldn't stop. By his senior year in high school he had become a class officer and editor of *Hi-Lite*, the Dickson yearbook. Though he had participated in various team sports, with his newfound voice, his heart was no longer in athletic competition. Instead, Jones channeled all his energies into oration, joining the school debate team and becoming a champion public speaker.

At graduation exercises Jones delivered the valedictory speech. It was a remarkable moment in his once-voiceless life. He was awarded the Regents Alumni College Scholarship and was accepted into the 1949 freshman class at the University of Michigan at Ann Arbor. These

The University of Michigan (c. 1940), where Jones first began to consider an acting career.

two honors prompted Mr. Daniels, the high school superintendent, to suggest that Jones share the good news with his parents. Mr. Daniels even gave James Earl the coins to make the calls from the pay phone in Sturdevant Market, the local drugstore in Brethren.

Like most farm dwellers, the Connollys didn't have a telephone at home. Jones had never used one before and didn't know how they worked. He entered and left the market several times, pacing up and down the street, too embarrassed to ask for help. Finally, he drove all the way to Manistee, where someone helped him place a call to New York City. He was calling his father, Robert Earl.

James Earl had never spoken with his father, and he didn't know what to expect. Though it was an awkward and brief conversation, Jones hung up the phone feeling that Robert Earl was pleased both by his news and their first contact.

With his uncle, Randy, James Earl was one of the first members of the family to attend college. Randy worked full-time and attended junior college in Grand Rapids until he had saved up enough money to enroll at the University of Michigan's engineering school. He earned his degree and went on to work for Boeing Aircraft. Mama and Papa were pleased with Randy's career choice.

James Earl, however, had occasionally thought about becoming an actor like his father. He remembered seeing, in an old issue of *Look* magazine, a photograph of Robert Earl with Mel Ferrer in the Broadway play *Strange Fruit*. His new command of language and his love of poetry and classic literature seemed to marry perfectly to a career in the performing arts, and he was impressed by his father's profession. But John Henry would hear none of it. His grandson would have to choose a practical profession, like law, medicine, or engineering.

In the fall of 1949 Jones began his college studies. To appease Papa, he chose the "pre-med" track, in preparation for a medical career. Perhaps because of all the years he had spent in silence, Jones kept to himself for the most part and did not socialize with other students. With a full schedule of classes and the part-time jobs he took to pay for the costs his Regents scholarship did not cover, he had little free time anyway. On Sundays Jones delivered the *Detroit Free Press* to students in the dormitories. He took work as a nude model for the Live Drawing classes in the University's Fine Arts department, and he took shifts manning the University's main switchboard—a significant accomplishment, since he had learned how to use a telephone only months earlier.

Jones's only real social interaction came from his participation in the Army's branch of the Reserve Officer Training Corps (the ROTC), which prepares college students to become officers in the United States Armed Services. Students who qualify for the program take military courses in addition to their regular school workloads. In return, these new officers are required to serve from six months to two years of active duty after graduation, depending on the current needs of the armed services branch under which they trained.

Jones poses with a University of Michigan classmate as they prepare for a performance of Aristophanes' The Birds. *The part of Epops was Jones's first real stage role.*

Although Jones studied diligently, his pre-med courses were extremely difficult. Nothing that he had studied in high school had prepared him for college-level chemistry or physics. He often felt overwhelmed by the amount of information that he was expected to absorb, and he finally decided that he was not cut out to be a doctor. Still attracted to and intrigued by a career in the arts, he began studying drama and enrolled in acting courses. He was determined to do something he enjoyed before being placed on active duty to fight in the latest international conflict, the Korean War.

The country of Korea lies between China and Japan, halfway around the world from the United States. The Japanese had occupied Korea for 50 years; the country was liberated in 1945 by the United States and the Union of Soviet Socialist Republics (U.S.S.R.). American troops were stationed in the southern part of the country, and Russian forces occupied the northern region, above the 38th parallel. Korea, once occupied—but unified—by an imperial government, was suddenly a country divided, partly democratic, partly Communist. On June 25, 1950, in an effort to unify Korea by force, Communist North Korea attacked South Korea. The United States and its allies immediately sent troops into South Korea. Within five months, Communist Chinese forces allied themselves with North Korea. In 1953, with the war already into its third year, Jones felt that it was only a matter of time before he would be called up to fight.

In the meantime, however, he auditioned for several campus plays. He won the role of Epops, the King of the Birds, in Aristophanes' *The Birds*. Next he landed the lead role in Arnaud d'Usseau and James Gow's *Deep Are the Roots*, a play about racial intolerance in the South. Soon Jones was getting parts in the off-campus Ann Arbor community theater, including the role of Verges in Shakespeare's *Much Ado About Nothing*. Amazingly, Jones never told his drama cast mates or his teachers about his stuttering problem. Not until years later, when Jones began to talk about his childhood as a stutterer, would people learn of his struggle.

In college Jones grew from a teenage boy into a man, becoming increasingly independent from his family. Along the way he had begun to make many decisions about the direction of his education and his career. The next big decision he faced involved his father. Robert Earl still wanted to see his son. He wanted him to come to New York for a visit. Jones, now 21, didn't need Papa and Mama's approval. He was free to make his own choices,

Among the many cultural attractions James Earl experienced during his first visit to New York were several opera performances, including Tosca, *shown here with Leontyne Price in the title role.*

and this time he would meet Robert Earl. On his way back from an ROTC encampment, Jones headed for New York.

Father and son greeted one another awkwardly at the train station, but soon Robert Earl relaxed somewhat and began telling his son how often he had tried—unsuccessfully—to see him. Robert Earl wanted to make this first visit special.

And it was. He showed his son everything he loved about New York culture: operas like *Tosca*, ballets like *Swan Lake*, and plays like *Pal Joey* and *The Crucible*. One night Robert Earl took his son to see a special actor at work. He introduced him to his friend, Paul Robeson.

A gifted singer and actor, Paul Robeson was one of the first truly successful international black performers. But in an era of anti-Communist sentiment, his outspoken views on racism, the rights of workers, and justice for the poor and the oppressed were not well received by most Americans. Even the U.S. State Department suspected him of being a Communist, a traitor, or a spy.

Eventually the entertainment industry itself ostracized Robeson. In a practice known as "blacklisting," those holding high positions in the industry singled out individuals whom they believed should not be hired because of their controversial political beliefs or affiliations. But Robeson would not be silenced. "I shall take my voice wherever there are those who want to hear the melody of freedom, or the words that might inspire hope and courage in the face of despair and fear," he defiantly declared.

Meeting Paul Robeson was a significant moment for James Earl Jones. Robeson was awe-inspiring as a man and electrifying as an actor. Robert Earl admired him greatly. In an era when black men in America had few opportunities to make their voices heard, Robeson's rang out loud and clear. Because Robert Earl shared Robeson's political views, using politics as the only outlet for his energies other than his own on-again, off-again career, he, too, was blacklisted. Years later James Earl's own theatrical career in many ways would match Robeson's: he would portray some of the same strong characters, for example, including Brutus in *The Emperor Jones* and the lead in *Othello*.

Jones's first visit with his father was strange and marvelous for both men. But though Robert Earl Jones may have hoped that his meeting with James Earl would be as father and son, for James Earl it was too late to begin forging that kind of relationship. The only way that he could relate to Robert Earl was as one man to another. Nevertheless, it was a beginning. The two would finally start fill-

Paul Robeson, one of the first truly international black American performers, was an outspoken advocate of workers' and civil rights. Jones's early encounter with Robeson would inspire him years later to take on the role of Robeson in the one-man stage performance written by Paul Hayes Dean.

ing the gaps left from their years of separation. Jones was at last becoming acquainted with the man who, until this trip, had been a stranger.

After four years of schooling, Jones left the university a few credits shy of graduating. He did not even bother to take his final exams at the end of his senior year. What would be the point? The Korean conflict was intensifying daily, and he was certain that his orders for active duty could come at any time. That summer Jones decided to go home to the farm in Dublin while he waited to be called.

With basic masonry, electrical, and carpentry skills, Jones found a part-time job on the stage crew at the Ramsdell Opera House, a community theater in Manistee. Housed in a turn-of-the-century theater, the troupe staged productions during the summer tourist season. Although the pay wasn't great, the opportunities were, as Jones later recalled:

I built and struck sets, worked lights, and worked as a stagehand, and later, as stage manager. I loved being part of a small fraternity of people doing something unusual together, creating something impossible out of something unseen. As a stage crew, we worked in privacy, at night, with no fanfare. What we did we did not advertise. I loved this community in the theater.

Soon Jones was feeling comfortable enough with his college and community theater experience to audition for a few minor roles. Mama and Papa still disliked the idea of James Earl becoming an actor, mostly because they associated acting with Robert Earl. However, they would drive to Manistee on many summer nights to watch their grandson's performances.

One such evening, July 27, 1953, news of a truce in Korea made its way backstage. Jones had avoided combat, but he was also without a college degree. By summer's end, with his commission as second lieutenant, he was ordered to report for active duty in Colorado. The primitive surroundings of the military base and the cold, harsh weather proved to be solid training in fitness and survival. Jones enjoyed the challenges, and he continued his love affair with nature and the outdoors.

Shortly before his tour of duty was over, Jones was promoted to first lieutenant. Pleased with his military skills and his competency as an officer, he now had to decide whether to extend his tour another two years and strive to make captain or to accept his discharge and return to civilian life. Uncertain about what he should do, he consulted his commanding officer, who asked him if there was anything he wanted to do "on the outside." Without hesitation Jones related his strong desire to try an acting career. The officer assured him that he could always return to the army if things didn't work out, and remembering the many words of encouragement from his high school teacher Donald Crouch, Jones decided to accept his discharge from the army. He was going to be an actor.

Joseph Papp (left) directs James Earl Jones, Nan Martin (center), and Bette Henritze (right) in a 1962 Shakespeare in the Park production of The Merchant of Venice.

6

"HITCH YOUR WAGON TO A STAR"

"Professor Crouch had encouraged me to keep reading Emerson. If you read enough Emerson, he promised, when you go into your adult life and choose your career, no matter what you do, you will do it well. If you understand Emerson, whatever you choose you will be your best."

—James Earl Jones, *Voices and Silences*

WITH HIS MILITARY tour of duty behind him, Jones headed home during the summer of 1955 to Dublin, back to the farm, back to Papa and Mama. Ultimately Jones wanted to take acting classes and earn his undergraduate degree. He returned to the Ramsdell Opera House, eager to resume his theater training and to gain further experience in pursuit of a successful acting career. There was plenty of work to do as the summer season approached, and once again Jones was involved in the technical work of live theater, building sets and managing other cast members. He was also acting again, in such popular summer stock productions as *Dial M for Murder* and *The Caine Mutiny*.

At the end of the season at the Opera House, Madge Skelly, the managing director of the theater, encouraged Jones to complete his degree through an extension program at the University of Michigan. With Skelly's assistance Jones also applied for admission to the American Theatre Wing in New York, and he was accepted not long after.

Jones was elated and told Robert Earl the news. At the very least, he thought, since Robert Earl had some professional acting experience, he might be able to offer his son some advice. Robert Earl and his third wife, Jumelle, had a tiny apartment in Greenwich Village, and they invited Jones to move in with them. James Earl accepted. At 24 he was giving up all that was familiar to him—the farm, the university, and the army—to pursue his dream of becoming an actor. That fall, with the money he saved from his stint in the army and his salary from the Opera House, Jones moved to New York. His tuition at the American Theatre Wing was covered under the GI Bill (the popular name for the Serviceman's Readjustment Act of 1944, which provided assistance to U.S. veterans).

James Earl Jones enrolled under the stage name of Todd Jones, fashioned after the black actor and singer Todd Duncan, but a year later Jones returned to using his given name. Although Robert Earl was known in theater circles, Jones was not reverting to his given name because he thought it would get him work. The decision was much more personal. James Earl had not known his birth father until he became an adult, but reclaiming his own name was a gesture toward validating his lineage.

Like studying for a medical degree, becoming an actor was not easy. Jones attended classes all day and worked nights and early mornings to pay his living expenses, sanding and refinishing floors with Robert Earl, working as a janitor, and making hundreds of submarine sandwiches at Morris's Sandwich Place. In spare moments, he studied and napped, repeating the routine each day.

The strain of living together took its toll on James Earl and his father. Living in such close quarters seemed to

magnify the unresolved emotions between father and son. In 1956 Jones moved out of Robert and Jumelle's apartment and into a small, cold-water flat without heat or electric services.

Despite personal difficulties Robert Earl and James Earl were able to relate well on another level—their shared passion for acting. During the times when they worked together Jones and his father discussed their craft. Robert Earl knew Shakespeare's works thoroughly, and the two men talked at great length about Shakespearean characters and plays. Robert Earl was especially fascinated with *Othello*. Often he would read Othello's lines while James Earl took the role of Iago. James Earl also became

Members of the American Theatre Wing, including actresses Kim Hunter (second from left) and Patricia Neal (far right) carry props and stage equipment during the organization's move to a new building. Shortly after his decision to become an actor, James Earl Jones was accepted into the ATW, which founded the Tony Awards in 1947.

Jones (rear center) in his first Broadway role, as Edward the butler in Sunrise at Campobello, *1958, starring Ralph Bellamy and Mary Fickett as Franklin D. and Eleanor Roosevelt.*

enchanted with the Moor and began to feel a kinship with this imaginary character, who was a stranger in a strange land. And because Robert Earl would probably never have the chance to play Othello in a major production, James Earl would feel an even greater urgency to do so himself. Winning the role of the Moor in *Othello* became one of the younger Jones's lifelong goals.

Over the next few years Jones continued his studies at the American Theatre Wing and attended workshops to hone his acting skills. He also worked with Nora Dunphee, a speech coach who helped him to fine-tune his speech clarity, and studied with Will Lee, an acting coach who based his teaching on the belief that good acting draws on one's own life experiences. As a former stutterer, Jones was struck by Lee's approach. To Jones, acting was truly very personal:

Because of my muteness, I approached language in a different way from most actors. I came at language standing on my head, turning words inside out in search of meaning, making a mess of it sometimes, but seeing truth from a very different viewpoint. In those years I spent in virtual silence, I developed a passion for expression. I do not believe that speech is a natural function for the human species. Therefore, any barrier to speech—stuttering, for instance—only intensifies the difficulty of an essentially unnatural process, the futility of words. But as I regained my powers of speech and began to use them as an actor, I came to believe that what is valid about a character is not his intellect, but the sounds he makes.

James Earl completed his studies at the American Theatre Wing in 1957. He was barely getting by on the money he earned from odd jobs between occasional theater roles when he got his first "break": he was cast as understudy to Lloyd Richards, who played the part of Perry Hall in the Broadway production *The Egghead*, starring Karl Malden and directed by Hume Cronyn.

Not until almost three years later, however, in the spring of 1960, would Jones make his first real acting breakthrough. One day Jones bumped into Joe Papp, one of his former teachers at the American Theatre Wing. The chance meeting could not have occurred at a better time. Jones had begun to have doubts about his decision to pursue a performance career, and Papp was about to launch a new theatrical project. He offered Jones summer employment playing the part of Michael Williams in Shakespeare's *Henry V*. Little did Jones know when he accepted Papp's offer that he would become part of one of the most historic ventures in the world of theater: the New York Shakespeare Festival, or what is popularly known as "Shakespeare in the Park."

Joseph Papp had founded the New York Shakespeare Festival six years earlier, with the goal of making theater more accessible to ordinary people. With the support and funding of several foundations, corporations, and govern-

The program cover for the 1960 performance of Jean Genet's play The Blacks. *James Earl Jones's costars included a number of performers who would also rise to prominence, such as Roscoe Lee Browne, Godfrey Cambridge, Cicely Tyson, Louis Gossett Jr., Billy Dee Williams, Abbey Lincoln, Max Roach, and Maya Angelou (shown here in center).*

ment agencies, he was able to realize his dream of establishing a permanent site in New York's Central Park, where theater lovers of all kinds could attend high-quality performances of classic comedies and tragedies. Papp made theater affordable as well: all performances are free, and people can watch and listen as they stroll through the park or take lunch breaks. From its opening on June 29,

1960, Shakespeare in the Park was a hit. Critic Arthur Gelb described the first production as a "vividly beautiful and rousingly paced pageant. . . . all dash and splendor and spectacle—just what Shakespeare ordered." James Earl Jones enjoyed the challenges of performing outdoors, competing with the din of traffic or the occasional roar of an airplane passing overhead.

Papp's project was part of a wave of off-Broadway theater that crested during the 1960s. In this flourishing atmosphere, aspiring actors and actresses discovered a wealth of opportunities. Blacks were especially eager to take advantage of such openings in the arts. America was just beginning to awaken to racial injustices and segregation, and blacks no longer felt limited to lesser or obscure roles while major parts were awarded to whites. Like other blacks, Jones welcomed the opportunity to explore new creative territory and to experiment and test the boundaries of his talents, where skin color would no longer hinder his professional growth.

After Jones's involvement with Shakespeare in the Park, acting roles began to come his way with more frequency. In 1961 he was cast in Jean Genet's controversial play *The Blacks*, whose all-black cast featured several future stars, including Cicely Tyson, Louis Gossett Jr., Billy Dee Williams, and Maya Angelou. The story line of the play tested the racial climate of the early 1960s. A "deceptively ironic" play, according to Jones, *The Blacks* appears to be carefully structured yet dissolves into "anarchy, chaos." He describes the play's plot:

Before an audience of masked figures—a queen and her valet, a judge, a governor, a missionary—a group of blacks perform[s] a ritualized murder. When the authority figures—representatives of white colonialism—set out to punish the murderers, they themselves are killed. This violent action is a ploy to divert the audience from a more somber offstage drama: a black is being tried and executed for betraying his people.

In a subtle casting twist, the white authority figures who intended to judge the blacks were actually black actors wearing stylized white masks—a striking reversal of the vaudevillian tradition of white performers' wearing blackface to play black characters. The play starkly reflected the real-life drama of race relations in America and the civil-rights movement's cry for an end to segregation.

As the '60s progressed, the political atmosphere in America, which was already undergoing explosive social and technical advances, would become increasingly volatile. In Southeast Asia, in a tiny country called Vietnam, U.S. military involvement grew deeper—and more unpopular—as years passed without a resolution to the conflict. The clashing ideologies of two superpowers, the United States and the U.S.S.R., intensified the Cold War and threatened to push the world to the brink of extinction with a nuclear war. At the same time, a black minister named Martin Luther King Jr. was espousing a peaceful social revolution, leading marches, demonstrations, and sit-ins. Widespread protests against racial discrimination and segregation in education, employment, the military, and public facilities awakened Americans to the fact that in many places, blacks were forbidden to eat in the same restaurants, use the same rest rooms, attend the same schools, or apply for the same jobs as whites. Waves of rioting swept the nation's cities, and in retaliation many of the bravest advocates of equality would become casualties in the race war. King, a tireless champion of the civil rights movement, would be murdered in 1968. President John F. Kennedy and his brother Senator Robert F. Kennedy would also lose their lives. The country would express its outrage over injustice in America through violence, then cry and mourn the losses brought on by such anger and hatred.

But there was a brighter side to the '60s. Music, film, and theater thrived in this tumultuous time of self-expression, and advances in research yielded scientific, medical,

Jones as Lieutenant Lothar Zogg in Dr. Strangelove, *his first film role.*

and technological milestones. By the end of the decade the world would witness humanity's first steps on the moon, transmitted into millions of homes through television.

Perhaps because *The Blacks* touched a nerve with so many viewers, Jones and his costars received encouraging reviews. *The New Yorker* called Jones "magnetic, but puzzling," questioning whether he was at ease onstage or had learned how to harness his own dramatic power. After *The Blacks* closed, Jones accepted other unusual and challenging roles, appearing in *Clandestine on the Morning Line*, for which he was awarded his first Obie, *The Apple*, and *Moon on a Rainbow Shawl*, in which he and Robert Earl worked together—and for which Jones earned Daniel Blum's Theatre World Award as Most Promising Personality. Around this time Jones had also begun to land minor TV roles. Clearly 1961 had become "his" year.

Following his award-winning year in theater was a similarly successful year in film. Jones was playing the Prince of Morocco opposite George C. Scott's Shylock in Joseph Papp's *The Merchant of Venice* when he attracted the attention of Hollywood director Stanley Kubrick. Kubrick was casting the movie *Dr. Strangelove* and had come to see Scott. After seeing Jones's performance, however, he offered him a role also, as Lieutenant Lothar Zogg. *Dr. Strangelove* was not only Jones's first experience in another performance medium, it was also his first trip abroad: the movie was filmed in Europe. Jones enjoyed his brief stay in London, but he missed his home and the stage and was eager to return.

After another successful summer with the New York Shakespeare Festival, Jones joined most of the original cast members of *The Blacks* for a return engagement to celebrate its 1,000th performance. The play had become the longest-running off-Broadway production in New York City. The success of *The Blacks* far exceeded the expectations of those who had been involved with the play when it opened two years earlier.

Jones was enjoying his great fortune. His career opportunities grew brighter with each new role he accepted, and
he was becoming more widely known with each performance. Shortly before Christmas 1963 he was interviewed
by *Newsweek* magazine. Calling Jones a "Dynamo" who
had appeared in 18 plays in 30 months, *Newsweek* noted
his powerful stage presence and his optimism:

> In play after play, [Jones] tromps on stage like a wild pony
> and, with a broad, irresistible grin, communicates his own
> pleasure at being there. Then he pounces upon the audi-
> ence with his thunderous voice. . . .
>
> Asked to project himself into his future, he stretches
> his imagination, smiles, and says: "I might even become
> a star."

"I will concede that I have a way of falling in love with my Desdemonas," Jones admitted in his autobiography. Here he appears with Julienne Marie in the 1964 New York Shakespeare Festival production of Othello, *for which Jones received his first Drama Desk-Vernon Rice Award. The two were married four years later.*

7

LIFE IMITATES ART

"I love to play renegades, rogues, and ramblers. They are not really bound by social trappings anyway. Race does not matter."

—James Earl Jones, *Voices and Silences*

EVERY ACTOR DREAMS of an opportunity to play a character that marks a defining moment in his or her career. James Earl Jones was fortunate enough to have three: Shakespeare's Othello; Jack Johnson, the first black heavyweight boxing champion; and the black actor Paul Robeson.

James Earl Jones had his first chance to portray Shakespeare's tragic hero in 1956 during his third summer season with the Ramsdell Opera House. This began a career-long fascination with the complex character. Years later Jones explained why:

> I have not yet solved the mystery of Othello, and I have played him many times, at different ages in my life. . . . [I have] at least a piece of the Othello puzzle, and it sustained what has been a lifelong interest in the brooding, majestic Moor, troubled by his betrayal at the hands of his

trusted friend Iago, obsessed with his wife Desdemona, torn by the dark conflicts of passion and revenge.

In some ways, Jones's life was similar to Othello's. The Moor is a black man in Italy, a foreigner in a strange land; Jones was a black actor in an industry dominated by whites. Othello marries Desdemona, a white woman; Jones fell in love with Pam Printy, a white woman who played Desdemona opposite him in the Manistee Theater production. The relationship was difficult for Jones and Printy: in a small midwest town in the 1950s, interracial romances were not widely accepted.

In Shakespeare's play, Othello's closest confidant, Iago, becomes jealous and angry over Othello's decision to promote Cassio to second-in-command of the Venetian forces. Iago contrives to make Othello believe that Cassio and Othello's wife, Desdemona, are having an affair—with tragic consequences. One of the primary themes of *Othello* concerns victims who are vulnerable to—and betrayed by—the people whom they trust the most. Perhaps another reason that Jones identifies with the character of Othello is that he may have experienced similar emotions as a child, when John Henry took him without explanation to Memphis with the intention of leaving him with his grandmother Elnora while the rest of the family moved. He certainly felt that way during the Manistee Theater production of *Othello* when his father Robert Earl told him that Pam Printy, with whom Jones had already become involved, had flirted with Robert Earl during a party they had all attended.

Societal attitudes about interracial relationships had changed little by 1964, when Jones finally realized his dream of playing Othello in a major production. Until then, only two black actors had ever done so. The first, Ira Aldridge, a 19th-century American actor, was permitted to play Othello in every country but his own. The only other black actor to carry the role on stage was Paul Robeson, the controversial and blacklisted star whom Jones had met

Sada Thompson (left), Julienne Marie (center), and James Earl Jones in the 1964 Shakespeare in the Park production of Othello.

during his first visit with Robert Earl in 1952. Knowing that he would be a pioneer of sorts only heightened Jones's own desire to play the Moor in a major production. He finally got his chance on Christmas Day, 1963, when Joe Papp offered Jones the part in the company's Central Park production to open the following summer.

Jones's stint with the New York Shakespeare Festival was his 10th production with the company and marked a milestone in his eight-year stage career. It was also in this time and place that he fell in love for the second time with his Desdemona, an actress named Julienne Marie, who would become Jones's first wife.

The play's director, Gladys Vaughn, encouraged Jones to play Othello without infusing the character with the rage over racism that was swirling all around them. By following her suggestion he was able to create a personality who appeared strong, noble, and compassionate, not dis-

Jones worked hard both mentally and physically to prepare himself for the role of Jack Jefferson in The Great White Hope. *In addition to beginning a strenuous exercise regimen, he also shaved his head (facing page) so that he would more closely resemble the great heavyweight boxer Jack Johnson (right), about whom the play was written.*

trustful or defensive, and his Othello was therefore more believable and appealing to the audience. Playing the role this way also gave Jones a clearer insight into the character that he had sought to understand for so long.

The Shakespeare Festival rehearsals began in March 1964, and the play opened in Central Park in July of the same year. After 19 performances, it traveled to Philadelphia for a brief run before opening off-Broadway in Octo-

ber at the Circle in the Square. At the end of the play's successful run, Jones was awarded the Drama Desk-Vernon Rice Award. In the December 11, 1964, issue of *Life* magazine, critic Tom Prideaux praised Jones's performance:

> This season has produced two major *Othellos*, one in London with Sir Laurence Olivier that is justly celebrated, the other in New York with the Negro actor James Earl Jones, that is unjustly neglected. . . . On the one hand, we have the far-famed and lavish London production—on the other a modest, obscure but truly remarkable show that began in Central Park last summer and moved downtown.
>
> The American *Othello*, for better or worse, is affected by our own contemporary state of history. The ancient story of a dark-skinned Moor married to a fair Venetian noblewoman has special meaning to us in 1964 as a drama of miscegenation [race mixing]. It reminds us, if only sub-

James Earl Jones as Jack Jefferson and Jane Alexander as Eleanor Backman in a stage performance of The Great White Hope. *In his autobiography, Jones notes that Alexander met with a great deal of hostility for portraying the white mistress of a black man. Ironically, Jones remarks, he and his wife, Julienne, did not have the same difficulties in their private lives.*

liminally, of civil rights and race relations. . . .

James Earl Jones, a fine actor, takes on the title role with an obvious sense of responsibility. He is representing the American Negro in a great role at a crucial time. As the Moor, he is tender, strong, jovial, patient, and, above all, intelligent. . . . I think Jones would do better, in the play's climactic scenes, to pull out the stops and blast forth as the powerful actor that he is. . . . My admiration for Olivier in no way lessens my admiration for James Earl Jones. . . . within the limit of his historical circumstance, he is immensely moving.

Although James Earl Jones would portray Othello four more times in his career, none of these would equal the significance of his 1964 performance. His run in the Shakespeare in the Park production was truly a professional and personal turning point.

During the production, Jones had captured the notice of director Edwin Sherin, who came backstage one night to introduce himself. The actor left an impression on Sherin. He saw in Jones an actor with seemingly boundless energy, the kind of energy he wanted someone to bring to the character of Jack Jefferson in a play he was casting called *The Great White Hope*. In 1967 Sherin sent Jones the script to read.

The fictional character of Jack Jefferson was based on the great black boxing champion of the early 20th century, Jack Johnson. The son of former slaves, Johnson grew up in the southern port town of Galveston, Texas. His parents were illiterate and struggled to survive in the harsh economic conditions of the times. He left school after completing the fifth grade to help support the family, usually by working on the busy harbor docks, where he loaded and unloaded ships' cargoes of cotton, lumber, and cottonseed oil. It was strenuous work, but it paid well. The dock was a rough place, though, and Johnson often found himself involved in some form of fisticuffs. He soon realized that there was money to be earned in fighting, and he began frequenting local boxing clubs to spar and learn the sport.

Johnson won the 1903 Negro Heavyweight Championship title by beating "Denver" Ed Martin. Despite his obvious skills, he would wait five more years to fight for the world title. Racial discrimination permeated the ranks of professional boxing during this period, and Johnson was prohibited from competing against whites. He finally earned a shot at the title in 1908, when he matched up against Tommy Burns, who was the current world champion. Johnson stunned the white-dominated world of boxing when he easily knocked out Burns to become the first black heavyweight champion of the world.

Jack Johnson was flamboyant, cocky, and defiant. He

romanced white women and toted them on his arm in public—unheard-of behavior at the time. He drove fast cars, wore expensive clothing, smoked cigars, drank champagne, and flaunted his extravagant lifestyle in front of white society. The professional boxing world was so offended by Johnson that it began searching for a "white hope," a boxer who could beat Johnson and reclaim the championship. Johnson's in-your-face attitude and his boxing talents were enough to back up his bravado for a time, but he would eventually lose both the heavyweight title and his wealthy celebrity lifestyle.

When James Earl Jones read Sherin's play about Johnson, he knew he had to take the part. Here was a story filled with drama, tragedy, and hope. It was the role of a lifetime. He also felt personally connected to the great boxer's story: he had recollections of John Henry's telling him about the great black boxing hero when he was a child, and as with Othello, Jones found in Johnson's life parallels to his own. Like Johnson's parents, Jones's great-great-grandfather Brice had been a slave. Johnson rose to prominence in a sport controlled by whites, and Jones had chosen a career in an industry dominated by whites. Both men had had romances with white women during times when such relationships provoked deep disapproval. And Jones's father had been a boxer before he became an actor.

Jones himself didn't look anything like a boxer, however, so he began a program of intense physical training to get himself in shape before opening night of *The Great White Hope*. He ran three miles every morning and then spent two hours in a gym skipping rope, pounding a body bag, and lifting weights to turn his actor's body into an athlete's. Jones watched every frame of film footage he could find on Johnson to get the feel of his boxing style. He even revived his own southern accent to sound more like him. Jones also read about Jack Johnson, looking for similarities between his life and that of other black men living in a racist society. He wanted to understand as much as he could about

James Earl Jones prepares for a performance of The Great White Hope *while the play's author, Howard Sackler, looks on.*

Jones in costume (above) for his role in the one-man stage performance based on the controversial life and opinions of Paul Robeson (facing page). Jones said that one of his reasons for wanting to play the title role in Paul Robeson *was for "all the young—and the not so young—people who had not been fortunate enough to know Paul Robeson even as little as I had."*

Johnson, both as a boxer/athlete and as man who forged a path to equality for American blacks.

By opening night at the Arena Stage in Washington, D.C., everyone involved with the play knew that they were part of something special. After 14 years of grabbing hold of every role he could to help him evolve as an actor, Jones himself was more than ready to step onstage as Jack Jefferson. What he wasn't prepared for was the critical acclaim for his performance, the rousing reception from the nightly audiences, or the fame that followed. "The acting is dominated by James Earl Jones, who is magnificent as Jefferson," enthused Clive Barnes of the *New York Times*. "With head shaved, burly, huge, Mr. Jones stalks through the play like a black avenging angel. Even when corrupted by misery, his presence has an almost moral force to it, and his voice rasps out an agony nearly too personally painful in its nakedness."

Another critic, Jerry Tallmer, declared, "Jones's performance as Jack Johnson in 'Great White Hope' has been rated the most exciting by an American actor since Marlon Brando first walked on in 1947 as the Stanley Kowalski of 'A Streetcar Named Desire.'"

Although one critic even called Jones an "overnight success," his fame had been anything but immediate. The once-mute child from Arkabutla, Mississippi, had worked long and hard to arrive at this professional moment.

In 1968 *The Great White Hope* moved to Broadway and earned even more acclaim. "Howard Sackler's play 'The Great White Hope' came into the Alvin Theater last night like a whirlwind, carrying with it, triumphantly, James Earl Jones," announced Barnes. "The play has an epic scope and range to it. . . . Mr. Jones was receiving a standing ovation of the kind that makes Broadway history." Jones turned in "a tidal wave performance," said critic Walter Kerr.

Jones won a Tony and a second Drama Desk-Vernon Rice award for his performance. His costar Jane Alexander was named Best Supporting Actress, and playwright Howard Sackler was honored with several awards, including the Pulitzer Prize for Drama and the New York Drama Critics' Circle Award.

Considering the tremendous success of the stage production, it wasn't surprising when Hollywood came knocking at the door with a film script of the story for both Jones and Alexander. Though the film version of *The Great White Hope* never achieved the success it had enjoyed on stage, Jones's performance earned him the only Academy Award nomination of his career.

Jones had been doing well, personally and professionally. But soon his life as an actor began to affect his relationship with Julienne. "For a time I lived in a golden haze of love and glory—and then my life seemed to tarnish at the edges and finally in the center. My life in the theater took its toll on my marriage," Jones would say. By the time Jones left for Barcelona, Spain, to finish filming *The Great White Hope*, he and Julienne had separated. Not long after, they divorced. Around the same time, Jones would face a professional crisis. He would step into a role that would put him in the middle of a disconcerting controversy.

James Earl Jones has always been vocal about his belief in the freedom of artistic interpretation in the arts. "There should be freedom in this society of ours for every writer, every screenwriter, every sculptor to express his or her own vision. I think our mission as artists is to shine our own light, the light of our own vision on any subject.

"I always want to fight for that right for the artist," Jones commented when he discussed the backlash he encountered as a result of portraying Paul Robeson.

Actor, singer, and activist Paul Robeson was the most controversial black performer of his time. Immensely talented and well educated, Robeson was an outspoken champion for the poor, the oppressed, and the needy, and he was openly critical about America's treatment of minorities. Unlike other civil-rights activists, however, he

Paul Robeson (center) greets his son, Paul Jr., and his daughter-in-law, Marilyn, at New York's JFK International Airport in 1963. Fiercely protective of his father's reputation, Paul Jr. worked hard to see that the play based on Robeson's life would not succeed.

believed that the Soviet Union's system of government offered greater equality for minorities than that of America. His outspokenness led many people to doubt his patriotism. After suffering the indignities of being blacklisted and forced to answer personal questions before various government committees, Robeson eventually became censured by blacks and whites alike. He lived out the last years of his life as a virtual outcast in America.

Upon his death in 1976, Robeson received enormous media coverage. America had long since overcome its fear of Communism, and it now realized that a great man had passed away. Not long after Robeson's death James Earl Jones, writer Paul Hayes Dean, and producer Don Gregory began work on a retrospective of his life. But there were those who resisted any attempt at such an endeavor, including Robeson's son, Paul Jr. The opposition intensified as the project neared completion.

Paul Robeson Jr. was very protective of his father's legacy. Because Robeson's life had been so complex and full of controversy yet at the same time so incredibly successful for a black professional, Paul Jr. believed that his father's life could easily be exploited or misrepresented. Should one present Robeson as hero, mentor, role model, or as antagonist, even traitor? Jones began to feel that no matter how the one-man play was written, Paul Jr. would not be satisfied that his father's life was being presented accurately. "He just did not want this show done," he said of Robeson's son. "I began to believe that Paul Jr. did not want actors, singers, artists, writers—anyone—to address his father's story. He considered himself the sole custodian of that image, a position that warrants some respect."

After the play opened Paul Jr. became a fixture outside the theater, picketing, protesting, and talking to any reporters who would listen. When the play moved on to another city, the protests outside continued. Paul Jr. enlisted the support of many prominent blacks, who formed an organization called the National Ad Hoc Committee to End Crimes against Paul Robeson, and he printed a protest statement in the preeminent trade magazine *Variety*. Among the 56 petitioners were civil-rights activist Coretta Scott King, authors James Baldwin and Maya Angelou, choreographer Alvin Ailey, and actor/activist Ossie Davis.

Jones was both stunned and hurt by the intensity and the source of the opposition, even more so after it became known that many of the signers had either not seen any of the performances or had had their names used without their consent. How could they truly know what kind of portrait Jones was painting of Robeson unless they saw it for themselves? Jones's motivation for taking the role had been twofold. First, like any other role he had taken on, playing Paul Robeson was a challenge, another "mountain to climb." Secondly, Jones wanted to bring Robeson's story and his work to other blacks, young and old, who had not known his achievements. In a time when there were no "real heroes," no "examples or alternatives," Paul Robeson was an epic hero.

Eventually Coretta Scott King and Ossie Davis did attend one of Jones's performances, and King met Jones backstage after the show to tell him that she admired his efforts in the play. Despite the furor outside the theaters in which *Paul Robeson* was being performed, the play was received favorably by audiences. Moreover, other prominent blacks, including Ruby Dee—the wife of one of the play's most vocal opponents, Ossie Davis—praised Jones in the *New York Amsterdam News*. Jones, she wrote, had "for a little while . . . giv[en] us a powerful picture of a powerful man who walked among us and sang and tried to fight some battles and to win some victories and by doing so to shore up our collective dignity as human beings."

By the time the play opened in New York in January 1978—nearly one and a half years after the play's premiere—it was obvious that it would not run much longer. The continuing controversy had made it difficult for the play's producers to book future engagements. After Jones's final performance on February 26, he felt compelled by these circumstances to step out of character for the first time in his career to address his audience. Standing before a respectfully quiet crowd, he said:

> I've felt my best defense of a play is to go on stage every performance and play the play within the limits of my talent and according to the dictates of my conscience as a citizen and as an artist. But my feelings are constantly awake to those conditions and issues that arise outside the production, and now that the play is over, I want to air some of those feelings with you. . . .
>
> In my twenty-one-year career as an actor, I've been caught in the cross fires of many artistic-social disputes, watching them escalate to the point of abuse to freedom of artistic interpretation. . . .
>
> As I ask no one to do anything for me, I beg artists and public alike to do something for themselves, first for our freedom (fight for more rather than less) to express and

interpret. What is the function of a playwright if not to give to an audience his special insight about the essence of a great hero? Deny that right to fulfill that function, and there is no point in being an artist. . . .

Every play at some point should be disturbing. . . .

I don't stand here on the stage to make people go out of the theater feeling *good* over *nothing*. I'd much rather let them go out of the theater *disturbed* over *something*.

And so I'll see you in a couple of years, as soon as I've found a play through which I can disturb you—Good night.

An original poster for the 1977 film Star Wars.

8

OTHER CHARACTERS AND VOICES

"'You have about forty different ways of sliding,' people used to say to Ty Cobb. 'How do you decide which way to slide?'

'I don't think about it, I just slide,' he answered.

So it is with an actor's voice. You hope you have worked so hard for so long that you don't have to become self-conscious and think about it. You just use it organically, as the instrument of your art.

—James Earl Jones, *Voices and Silences*

"A LONG TIME AGO, in a galaxy far, far away. . . .

"It is a period of civil war. Rebel spaceships, striking from a hidden base, have won their first victory against the evil Galactic Empire.

"During the battle, Rebel spies managed to steal secret plans to the Empire's ultimate weapon, the Death Star, an armored space station with enough power to destroy an entire planet.

"Pursued by the Empire's sinister agents, Princess Leia races home aboard her starship, custodian of the stolen plans that can save her people and restore freedom to the galaxy. . . ."

This is the opening that young producer/director George Lucas wrote for his sci-fi adventure motion picture *Star Wars*. Filled with high-tech special effects and fantasy space creatures, the movie dazzled audiences young and old and broke box-office revenue records in the process. James Earl Jones's involvement with the project would add yet another dimension to his multifaceted career in a way that he would not have imagined only a few years earlier.

Although it was the first episode to be made into a film, *Star Wars: A New Hope*, released in 1977, was actually the fourth in a series of nine planned chapters of the famed "epic tale of Galactic Civil War." The story line concerns the themes of falling from grace and of conflict between good and evil forces, with characters masterfully created to fill each role. One such character was Darth Vader, Dark Lord of the Sith. Anakin Skywalker (Vader's name before he turned to the Dark Side) had once been a student of Obi-Wan Kenobi, a master of the Jedi, or space warriors. Skywalker grew impatient with Obi-Wan Kenobi's teachings. The evil Emperor Palpatine offered Skywalker a faster path to glory—the Dark Side, where in order to achieve mastery, one must give in to one's anger, fear, and aggression. Greedy and anxious for such powers, Skywalker allowed those feelings to envelop him and he became Darth Vader.

This futuristic "Prince of Darkness" looked as ominous as his essence. A commanding presence, he was tall and strong. Due to a near-fatal battle with Obi-Wan Kenobi, Vader's body was encased in an all-black armor suit with a black flowing cape attached. His mechanically assisted breathing echoed through his armored mask.

While searching for an actor who could carry such a role, Lucas thought of a British actor he knew, David Prowse, a six-foot seven-inch former weightlifter whom Lucas had seen play Frankenstein in several low-budget

British films. He offered Prowse the role of either Darth Vader or Chewbacca, another tall, imposing character who is affiliated with the "forces of good." Reminded by fellow actor friends that audiences always remember the villain, Prowse chose the role of Vader. Lucas agreed but knew that Prowse's Welsh accent was not suitable for the Dark Lord. The Vader character "required a deep, commanding voice to communicate the menace of his character," Lucas believed. Remembering James Earl Jones's resonant baritone voice, which had translated well to the characters he portrayed onstage and in film, Lucas decided to approach him to create Vader's voice.

James Earl Jones poses with a costume of Darth Vader that was presented to Planet Hollywood during an opening of one of its restaurants. During the opening Jones, who provided the voice-over for the Star Wars *film character, also received the 1993 Piper-Heidsieck Award, which is presented annually by the Chicago International Film Festival.*

King Mufasa (center), the ruler of the Pride Lands, is surrounded by Uncle Scar and his hyena henchmen, a warthog named Pumbaa, a meerkat named Timon, and his own son Simba in a publicity picture for the Disney film The Lion King. *Jones not only enjoyed recording the voice of Mufasa, but he also appreciated the film's strong father-and-son theme.*

When Jones's recorded voice was electronically modulated in the recording studio it sounded even more powerful. For Jones the movie offered another opportunity to stretch the boundaries of his talents, creating the sound presence of a character without physically performing the role. He had done numerous voice-over parts in his career, such as those in *King: A Filmed Record . . . Montgomery to Memphis* in 1970 and *Malcolm X* in 1972, but they had been narrations.

For his participation in *Star Wars*, Jones was paid $10,000, and he refused screen credit, perhaps because he enjoyed the idea of being an anonymous yet powerful voice. In his autobiography he explains the unexpected results of his work:

> For a long time I denied that I was Darth Vader's voice because it was fun to deny it. . . .
>
> The role set off a chain reaction of voices in my career. With Darth Vader, that mythical character, my voice came to be used more and more frequently as a voice of authority. It brought me a lot of commercial and voice-over work. The voice-over work led to more and more opportunities for narrations and on-camera commercials, with their own milieu and craft so different from movies and theatre.

Jones would be called upon to reprise the voice role in the two *Star Wars* sequels: *The Empire Strikes Back*, released in 1980, and *The Return of the Jedi*, released in 1983.

Nearly 10 years later Jones would land a voice-over part in an entirely different type of film—an animated feature. In 1994 Walt Disney Pictures released its 32nd full-length animated film, *The Lion King*. More than 600 artists, animators, and technicians worked on the project, generating more than one million drawings, including 1,197 hand-painted backgrounds and more than 100,000 frames of colored film.

What distinguishes this film from many of Disney's previous animated classics is its original story line. The African plains setting of the film provides the backdrop for the numerous animal characters who come to life through animation and through the voices of an ensemble of Hollywood talents. James Earl Jones was one of those talents. He would be the voice of Mufasa, the mighty lion king of the jungle.

The project became an "exciting adventure" for Jones, as he related in a publicity interview. "Doing a voice for animation is acting in its purest form," he said. "It's a bit like the ancient Greek form where the actors would wear masks. In our case, the masks are the animator's drawings and we just simply supply all the behaviors, emotions and

Jones (left) with his wife Ceci and their son, Flynn Earl. "My father passed on the legacy of the absent father," Jones says in his autobiography. "My mission has been to break that chain in my own life . . . I will always be there for my son."

feelings behind that mask." He went on:

> One of the reasons that I took this job was because of the impression the drawings and animation had on me. It was really grand stuff. I also enjoy creating characters with just my voice. . . . It's interesting to experiment and try it different ways until you get the right sound. I love the drama in the film and the way it resonates on other classic dramatic pieces such as Shakespeare's 'Hamlet.'

The supervising animator, Tony Fucile, was delighted to have Jones to help create the character of Mufasa:

> James Earl Jones was perfect for this part. I can't even imagine anyone else doing the voice [of Mufasa]. He adds

the regal quality that we needed and, on top of that, he's got this fatherly warmth that comes across. It was up to us to visually come up to that standard that he set with his voice. . . . Mufasa's animation is very subtle and there are times where he doesn't move but says a lot with just a stare. Each drawing has to say a lot and have a strong attitude.

Director Roger Allers was astounded at the strength of Jones's voice. "He has this incredibly huge and masterful voice that just resonated throughout the recording studio. Even without a microphone, it just filled the entire room." To make Mufasa sound even more majestic, however, Allers and codirector Rob Minkoff placed six microphones around Jones's head "so that the voice would surround you and sound like it was coming from everywhere."

Jones not only loved the process of recording for animation, but he also found the project enjoyable because of its subject matter. *The Lion King*, Jones said, is "the story of the enduring bond forged between a father and a son—a bond so strong that it transcends even the father's death. . . . [W]hat remains for the young Lion Prince Simba is a legacy of memories and strong principles, as taught him by his father, and those principles guide him toward his future." Perhaps it also reminded the actor of the strong and loving guidance he received from Papa and the acting advice that Robert Earl gave him in New York.

Because David Prowse had worn a mask as Darth Vader in *Star Wars*, there was no need for lip-synching accuracy, and it was not difficult for the sound engineers to dub Jones's voice onto the sound track of the film. Voice-over work for animation is a different process, however. Instead of "replacing" one voice with another, the actor is "creating" the voice, the persona that brings the character to life. For the most part, the actors in *The Lion King*—including Jonathan Taylor Thomas, Whoopi Goldberg, Nathan Lane, Cheech Marin, and Jeremy Irons—recorded their lines without other actors present, while an off-camera assistant read the lines of the other characters in the scene. In order to inject some of the actor's personality into Mufasa, the producer filmed Jones's facial expressions and body movements as he spoke his lines. The animators then incorporated some of those gestures into their individual drawings.

Jones's performance in *Star Wars* and *The Lion King* once again proved his versatility and his ability to adapt to any acting project. Though he is most comfortable onstage, he has never limited his career choices to theater roles—and he has succeeded in many other media. Until the early 1970s, however, he had worked mostly onstage or in films and only occasionally in television. Most of his TV roles had been cameo or guest appearances and narrations, but even in that medium he had broken new ground. His credits were impressive: in 1965 Jones was the first black actor to land a recurring role in a soap opera, as Dr. Jerry Turner in *As the World Turns*. He had also hosted a variety show called *Black Omnibus*, which featured interviews with black men and women in the arts, sports, politics, and other fields. This project was particularly challenging for Jones because of the more relaxed dialogue of conversation. He worried that his stuttering would return because he wasn't working with the aid of a prepared script. The show did not run long, but Jones nevertheless enjoyed the experience of having worked on a weekly series.

Several times in his career, James Earl Jones had been approached about starring in his own television drama series, but the timing or the projects themselves had never seemed right. That changed in 1979 when producer Steven Bochco created *Paris* with Jones in mind to play the lead character. Jones had known Bochco for years; Steven's mother, Mimi, was Jones's agent. The series concept, featuring a black police captain and detective, appealed to Jones.

Unfortunately, as with *Black Omnibus*, the program was short-lived, lasting only 13 weeks. Bochco attributed the

Laila Robins as defense attorney Victoria Heller and James Earl Jones as Gabriel Bird in the award-winning television series Gabriel's Fire. *The role earned Jones the first Best Actor Emmy Award of his career.*

failure to an audience that was not yet ready to watch a black man asserting authority over whites. But Jones felt otherwise. "On the contrary," he said, "I think we failed because we blew it—unsatisfactory stories and an unworkable one-character concept. . . . We should admit poor quality when *that* is the problem." Although *Paris* was not a commercial success, it marked a milestone: along with actor and colleague Louis Gossett Jr., who had also starred in his own show that year, Jones was one of the first blacks to star in a network television drama series.

For Jones there was also a more personal significance to the show: Cecilia Hart. When Bochco was casting *Paris*, he had offered a part in the show to Cecilia (called "Ceci"). At the time, she was married to Bochco's friend Bruce Weitz, who would later star in Bochco's successful police show *Hill Street Blues*. Jones was comfortable around Ceci, and they became fast friends on the set of *Paris*. After the show was canceled they stayed in touch, and after Ceci's marriage to Weitz ended, she and Jones began to date.

By 1981 the two were spending most of their time together, and Jones was in love. He knew he wanted to marry again, and he desperately wanted to have children. He was enjoying another successful run as *Othello* on Broadway and was feeling secure in his career and in his personal life. He wooed Ceci until she agreed to marry him. They held the wedding ceremony on March 15, 1982, while Jones had the afternoon off from the play. Eventually Ceci also joined the cast, and in a replay of earlier events in Jones's life, she played Desdemona. This time, however, his Desdemona was already his wife in real life. Nine months after they married, when Jones was nearly 52, Ceci gave birth to Flynn Earl Jones.

With a wife and child in his life, Jones's career priorities began to change. When Flynn was a toddler the family was free to travel to location shoots wherever Jones's projects took him. Once Flynn started school, however, Jones wanted to stay closer to home. Though *Paris* had not lasted long, Jones liked the experience enough to continue looking for another television series opportunity. It came in the form of *Gabriel's Fire*, a drama series about a Chicago cop who has spent 20 years in prison for killing his partner.

Jones was intrigued by the lead character, Gabriel Bird, and was challenged by the character's great potential to develop and evolve as the series progressed:

Suddenly, after twenty years of being locked away, [Bird] is ejected from the prison world into the real world, a world which has changed drastically since his incarceration began. While he has heard and read about this world and witnessed its transformations on television, he must now confront it in all its true unpredictability. . . . Running through the drama was an inescapable theme—the syndrome of incarceration, from the time of slavery up until today. There were rich psychological, sociological, and historical reverberations to explore.

Gabriel's Fire debuted on September 12, 1990. Running against two of the top-rated programs of the season, *The Cosby Show* and *The Simpsons*, the new show's ratings were low. However, the critics loved it, and both Jones and costar Madge Sinclair ultimately won Emmys for their performances that first season—for Jones, the first Best Actor Emmy Award of his career.

The program was reworked and renamed *Pros & Cons* for the 1991–92 season, and veteran actor Richard Crenna joined the cast. The show fared no better in the ratings, though, and was canceled halfway through its second season. In the final analysis, Jones believes that *Gabriel's Fire*, unlike *Paris*, had all the elements essential for a successful television series: strong writing, a good cast, and multidimensional characters. But he learned that television is more strongly influenced by its sponsors—and the results of poor ratings are more immediate—than theater or motion pictures. He has taken minor roles and has made guest appearances in other TV series, such as *Picket Fences* (1992), *Lois & Clark* (1993), and *Touched by an Angel* (1994), and in 1997 appeared in the Hallmark special *What the Deaf Man Heard*. But the longevity that Jones achieved onstage and in film did not carry into his television work. His powerful voice and strong presence were perhaps better suited for larger media formats.

As he had always done, Jones would keep moving.

A scene from August Wilson's play Fences, 1987. *For his role as Troy Maxson, Jones won his second Tony Award for Best Actor, as well as the prestigious once-in-a-lifetime Drama League Award. From left to right: Charles Brown, James Earl Jones, Mary Alice, and Ray Aranha.*

9

ALL THE WORLD'S A STAGE

"There is nothing more moving or powerful than the power of the Word when beautiful language is married to deep passion. The voice is the instrument for the expression of that power. Emotion is resultant, responsive. Passion is active, aggressive."

—James Earl Jones, *Voices and Silences*

THROUGHOUT JAMES EARL Jones's career, the theater has always been his home. He has often said that his film and television roles have paid the bills but that the theater, the stage, the audience, the immediacy of live performance are what fulfill him artistically.

After reading Howard Sackler's *The Great White Hope* in 1967, Jones was so galvanized by the character of Jack Jefferson that he knew it was a role he had to play. The critical and popular response validated Jones's belief in the power of the fictionalized boxing star. Now, 20 years later, it was only fitting that Jones's passionate commitment to the stage should culminate in the role of Troy Maxson in August Wilson's critically acclaimed play *Fences*.

Jones as Troy Maxson in Fences. *Playwright August Wilson said that the character of Maxson was written with Jones in mind. Despite Jones's love of the theater, after* Fences *closed he announced that he would limit his stage performances.*

For Jones it was as though the lightning of good fortune had struck twice. *Variety* magazine called Jones's portrayal of Troy Maxson "his best role since the career-elevating 1968–69 'The Great White Hope,' and indeed one of the best roles in any American play in recent memory." Jones's stunning performance, said the *New York Times*, established him as "America's premier black actor, a status yet to be challenged." The fact that Jones seemed to fit the part perfectly was no accident: playwright August Wilson "heard" Jones's voice while writing the character and had him in mind from the play's inception.

Set in an industrialized northeastern city in 1957, *Fences* tells the tale of an illiterate, middle-aged ex-con who once played baseball for the Negro Leagues. Maxson retains a sense of family and responsibility despite his deep-seated bitterness over the racial prejudice that prevented him from playing in the major leagues. Conflict arises when Maxson's son, Cory, is offered an athletic scholarship. Maxson forbids him to take it, a judgment that is clouded by his own selfishness and sense of failure as a man, a husband, and a father.

Once again, Jones's fascination with the humanness of a character drew him to the role. Maxson is anonymous America, a lower-middle-class worker with little education but a family to support. "Troy is supposed to jostle you, frighten you, and maybe even depress you," Jones said in an interview with Helen Dudar of the *New York Times*. "He ravages, partly because of his appetite, partly because he cannot separate his principles from his prejudices. . . . He wounds and bruises his kin. As an actor, I love him, just as I loved Jack Jefferson in 'Great White Hope.'"

To critics and audiences, Jones's love for his character was clearly evident. In its April 1, 1987, issue, *Variety* magazine praised his performance and his talent:

> [M]ake no mistake, this is James Earl Jones' play and a triumph for one of the most gifted actors of the American stage at the height of his art. His hulking body, basso voice, sly grin and daunting frown are the physical externals of a performance lit by an inner fire of conviction. It shakes the audience as only great stage acting can.

For his performance in *Fences* James Earl Jones earned his second Best Actor Tony. He also received the Drama League Award for the most distinguished performance of the 1986–87 season, an honor that is granted only once in an actor's lifetime. Perhaps his finest stage performance,

Fences may also be his last. "I no longer have the physical energy or the psychic stamina to sustain a Broadway run of a year," Jones said in 1993. "I no longer have it in me to play a role on stage . . . as much as I love the theater, as much as it is my real home."

Fences was not only one of Jones's best and most acclaimed performances, but it was also one of his favorites. And although he is most comfortable on the stage, many of his best-loved performances have been in film. Among them are those in *Soul Man*, *Matewan*, and *Field of Dreams*. It is "the simple films that tell a simple story with an ensemble cast" that Jones has preferred. At times he has taken roles largely for the opportunity to work with "rising stars" like Alec Baldwin and Jodie Foster or with veteran actors whom he admires, like Sean Connery, Sidney Poitier, and Robert Redford. In *Field of Dreams*, for example, Jones valued the experience of working with the legendary film actor Burt Lancaster as well as with Kevin Costner, at the time a young star.

Acting before the camera may be far different from performing on stage, but for Jones it is just as challenging. In his autobiography he compares the two mediums in this way:

> On the stage, the actor's job is to fill the whole space with sound, movement, emotion, animal presence, and energy. The simpler the character, the better on stage. On film, just the opposite is true. The acting must be subtle and suggestive. Film is far more subliminal than theatre, depending on imagery more than on words. I love the magic of film—the interplay of truth and illusion.

Jones has moved away from the theater, but he continues to work in film, appearing in such recent movies as *Cry, the Beloved Country* (1995), *A Family Thing* (1996), *Second Civil War*, a Home Box Office made-for-cable movie (1997), and *Gang Related* (1997), starring the late rapper and actor Tupac Shakur.

As though these projects did not keep him busy enough,

Jones (left) as Father Stephen Kumalo with Leleti Khumalo (center) in Darrell James Roodt's 1995 film adaptation of Alan Paton's novel Cry, the Beloved Country.

in 1995 James Earl Jones signed a contract making him the exclusive spokesperson for Bell Atlantic, a regional communications corporation, after a six-year affiliation with the company. Jones's "voice of communication" has become synonymous with Bell's tag line, "The Heart of Communication."

James Earl Jones, a once-silent child, has forged a remarkable career in a field where oration and articulation are essential. His achievements, both personal and professional, are a testament to that determination. At 67 years old, in the 41st year of his distinguished career, Jones has no immediate plans to retire. "I have the illusion that I am timeless," he admits. "I think of relinquishment, but not retirement. At some point I am going to give up a lot of commitments that, in the past, I have made almost reflexively. I am going to make a deeper connection to the country. I find more and more fulfillment there, in the house and the land and the family."

APPENDIX

FAMOUS PEOPLE WHO STUTTER

James Earl Jones is not alone in having overcome stuttering, or "dysfluency." Many leaders and celebrities throughout history—from athletes to artists, from scientists to singers—have also struggled with speech problems. Some of the most well-known figures include:

Aesop, Greek author of fables

Walter Annenberg, philanthropist

Clara Barton, founder of the American Red Cross

Lewis Carroll, author of *Alice's Adventures in Wonderland*

Winston Churchill, prime minister of Great Britain

Charles Darwin, naturalist and author of *The Origin of Species*

Lester Hayes, All-Pro Oakland/L.A. Raiders lineman

Bo Jackson, pro football and baseball player

Tommy John, pitcher for the New York Yankees

Greg Louganis, Olympic gold medal diver

Robert Merrill, opera singer

Marilyn Monroe, actress

Moses, Hebrew prophet

Sir Isaac Newton, scientist who discovered the laws of gravity

Carly Simon, pop singer

Jimmy Stewart, actor

Mel Tillis, country-and-western singer

John Updike, novelist

Ken Venturi, U.S. Open champion golfer

Bruce Willis, actor

Widely regarded as one of the greatest orators of the 20th century, Britain's Prime Minister Winston Churchill (right), shown here with President Franklin D. Roosevelt, was also a stutterer. He would prepare and rehearse his public addresses well in advance, and before each speech he would hum quietly to relax his vocal cords.

STUTTERERS PORTRAYED IN FILMS, TELEVISION, AND VIDEO*

The Right Stuff (film, 1983)

A Fish Called Wanda (film, 1988)

Glory (film, 1989)

It (television miniseries, 1990)

Quantum Leap (television, two episodes, 1993)

Color of Night (film, 1994)

Leaving Minnesota (film, 1996)

A Family Thing (film, 1996)

Moses (television, 1996)

Smilla's Sense of Snow (film, 1997)

Speaking of Courage (video, n.d.)

Voices to Remember (video, n.d.)

BOOKS ABOUT STUTTERING**

Brown, Alan, and Grant Forsberg. *Lost Boys Never Say Die*. New York: Delacorte Press, 1989.

Bunting, Eve. *Blackbird Singing*. New York: Macmillan Publishing, 1980.

Chambers, Aidan. *Seal Secret*. New York: Harper and Row, 1980.

Holland, Isabelle. *Alan and the Animal Kingdom*. Philadelphia: Lippincott, 1977.

Stucley, Elizabeth. *The Contrary Orphans*. New York: Franklin Watts, 1961.

Westbrook, J., and J. Ahlbach. *Listen with Your Heart*. Anaheim Hills, Ca.: National Stuttering Project, 1996.

OTHER RESOURCES

Hollins Communication Research Institute
P.O. Box 9737
Roanoke, VA 24020
(540) 362-6528
Fax: (540) 362-6663
E-mail: adm-hcri@rbnet.com

National Stutterers' Hotline
1-800-221-2483 (United States and Canada)

National Stuttering Project
5100 East La Palma Avenue, Suite 208
Anaheim Hills, CA 92807
1-800-364-1677
Fax: (714) 693-7554
E-mail: nspmail@AOL.com

Stuttering Foundation of America
P.O. Box 11749
3100 Walnut Grove Road, #603
Memphis, TN 38111
1-800-992-9392
E-mail: stuttersfa@AOL.com

* Source: "Famous People Who Stutter." http://www.casafuturatech.com/
** Source: "Just for Kids: A Special Page for Kids Who Stutter."
    http://www.mankato.msus.edu/dept/comdis/kuster/kids/kids.html

James Earl Jones as host of the 1998 public television series Long Ago & Far Away, *which introduced children to the art of storytelling.*

CHRONOLOGY

1931   James Earl Jones born on January 17 in Arkabutla, Mississippi

1936   Grandfather John Henry Connolly sells the farm in Mississippi and moves the family north to Manistee, Michigan. Shortly after, James Earl begins to stutter

1949   Graduates from Dickson High School, earns Regents Alumni Scholarship, and enrolls at the University of Michigan in Ann Arbor

1955   Moves to New York City and attends the American Theater Wing

1960   Joins the New York Shakespeare Festival, or "Shakespeare in the Park"

1962   Wins Obie Award for Best Actor in the off-Broadway *Clandestine on the Morning Line* and Theatre World Award for Most Promising Personality

1965   Wins Obies for *Baal* and *Othello*

1968   Marries Julienne Marie (they divorce some time after 1971)

1969   Wins Tony Award for Best Actor in *The Great White Hope*

1977   Records the voice of Darth Vader in *Star Wars*

1982   Marries Cecilia Hart; son Flynn is born

1985   James Earl's mother, Ruth Connolly Jones, dies at age 75

1987   Wins Tony Award for Best Actor in *Fences*

1989   Begins recording commercials for Bell Atlantic

1991   Wins Emmy for Best Actor in a drama series for *Gabriel's Fire* and Best Supporting Actor for his role in the Turner Network Television movie *Heat Wave*

1992   Receives the National Medal of the Arts

1995   Signs contract to be exclusive spokesperson for Bell Atlantic

1997   Appears in feature film *Gang Related* with Tupac Shakur

FURTHER READING

Angelou, Maya. *I Know Why the Caged Bird Sings*. New York: Bantam Books, 1971.

Arnold, Christine. "James Earl Jones: A New Standard for Othello." *Philadelphia Inquirer,* December 30, 1981.

Bobrick, Benson. *Knotted Tongues: Stuttering in History and the Quest for a Cure*. New York: Simon & Schuster, 1995.

Donlon, Brian. "Jones' Slice of Emmy Pie." *USA Today*, August 27, 1991.

Dudar, Helen. "James Earl Jones at Bat." *New York Times, Arts and Leisure*, March 22, 1987.

Dutka, Elaine. "Color Doesn't Bind You—It Just Lumps You Together: Q & A with James Earl Jones." *Los Angeles Times*, December 19, 1995.

Ehrlich, Scott. *Paul Robeson: Singer and Actor*. New York: Chelsea House, 1988.

Hauser, Pierre. *The Community Builders: 1877–1895*. New York: Chelsea House, 1996.

Henry, Christopher. *Forever Free: 1863–1875*. New York: Chelsea House, 1995.

Hine, Darlene Clark. *The Path to Equality: 1931–1947*. New York: Chelsea House, 1995.

Jakoubek, Robert. *Jack Johnson: Heavyweight Champion*. New York: Chelsea House, 1990.

Jones, James Earl. *James Earl Jones: With a Strong Voice*. Produced and directed by Alan J. Weiss. 50 min. Alan Weiss Productions, Inc., 1995. Videocassette.

Jones, James Earl and Penelope Niven. *Voices and Silences*. New York: Simon & Schuster, 1993.

Leahy, Michael. "Gabriel's Ire." *TV Guide*, October 27, 1990.

Longfellow, Henry Wadsworth. *The Song of Hiawatha*. New York: Bounty Books, 1982.

Miramax Films. *Cry, the Beloved Country*. Miramax Films, 1995. Press Kit.

Pollock, Dale. *Skywalking: The Life and Films of George Lucas*. Hollywood: Samuel French Trade, 1990.

Rosenfeld, Megan. "James Earl Jones Is Enjoying His First Child, and a Good Role." *Philadelphia Inquirer*, April 21, 1983.

Shirley, David. *Alex Haley: Author*. New York: Chelsea House, 1994.

Sisson, Mary. *The Gathering Storm: 1787–1829*. Philadelphia: Chelsea House, 1997.

Walt Disney Company. *The Lion King*. The Walt Disney Company, 1994. Press Kit.

FILMOGRAPHY

Selected Theater, Film, and Television Appearances

THEATER

The Egghead (1957)

Henry V (1960)

The Blacks (1961)

Clandestine on the Morning Line (1961)

Romeo and Juliet (1961)

A Midsummer Night's Dream (1961)

Moon on a Rainbow Shawl (1961)

The Merchant of Venice (1962)

The Tempest (1962)

Macbeth (1962)

Othello (various performances
    from 1963 through 1982)

Emperor Jones (1964)

Baal (1965)

Of Mice and Men (1967)

The Great White Hope (1967–68)

Hamlet (1972)

The Cherry Orchard (1973)

King Lear (1973)

Paul Robeson (1977)

Hedda Gabler (1980)

Master Harold . . . and the Boys (1982)

Fences (1987)

FILMS AND VIDEOS

Dr. Strangelove, or How I Learned to Stop Worrying and Love the Bomb (1963)

The Great White Hope (1970)

King: A Filmed Record . . . Montgomery to Memphis, narrator (1970)

Malcolm X, narrator (1972)

Bingo Long Traveling All-Stars and Motor Kings (1976)

The Greatest Thing That Almost Happened (1977)

Star Wars, voice (1977)

The Empire Strikes Back, voice (1980)

Return of the Jedi, voice (1983)

Soul Man (1986)

Matewan (1987)

Gardens of Stone (1987)

Coming to America (1988)

Field of Dreams (1989)

The Hunt for Red October (1990)

Patriot Games (1992)

Sneakers (1992)

The Meteor Man (1993)

Sommersby (1993)

The Sandlot (1993)

The Lion King, voice (1994)

Clear and Present Danger (1994)

Cry, the Beloved Country (1995)

Jefferson in Paris (1995)

Looking for Richard (1996)

A Family Thing (1996)

Gang Related (1997)

TELEVISION

The Defenders (1964)

As the World Turns, series (1965)

Dr. Kildare (1966)

Tarzan (1967–68)

N. Y. P. D. (1969)

Black Omnibus, series host and narrator (1973)

Jesus of Nazareth (1977)

Roots II: The Next Generation (1979)

Paris (1979–80)

Guyana Tragedy: the Story of Jim Jones (1980)

Highway to Heaven (1986)

L.A. Law (1988)

Long Ago and Far Away, series host (1989)

Gabriel's Fire (1990)

Heat Wave (1990)

Pros and Cons, formerly *Gabriel's Fire* (1991)

JFK Conspiracy (1992)

Percy and Thunder (1992)

Lincoln, narrator (1992)

Picket Fences (1992)

Race for Life: Africa's Great Migration, narrator (1993)

Lois and Clark (1993)

Touched by an Angel (1994)

What the Deaf Man Heard (1997)

Jones as Mr. Moses in MGM's adventure comedy The Meteor Man, *1993.*

INDEX

PICTURE CREDITS

Judy L. Hasday, a native of Philadelphia, Pennsylvania, received her B.A. in communications and her Ed.M. in instructional technologies from Temple University. A multimedia professional, she has had her photographs published in several magazines and books, including a number of Chelsea House titles. She enjoys classical music, travel, and collecting first-edition books.

James Scott Brady serves on the board of trustees with the Center to Prevent Handgun Violence and is the Vice Chairman of the Brain Injury Foundation. Mr. Brady served as Assistant to the President and White House Press Secretary under President Ronald Reagan. He was severely injured in an assassination attempt on the president, but remained the White House Press Secretary until the end of the administration. Since leaving the White House, Mr. Brady has lobbied for stronger gun laws. In November 1993, President Bill Clinton signed the Brady Bill, a national law requiring a waiting period on handgun purchases and a background check on buyers.